LEARN TO
Quilt With Panels

Country Bears, page 54

www.companyscoming.com
visit our website

Front Cover: Corner Cabins, page 24

Learn to Quilt With Panels

Copyright © Company's Coming Publishing Limited

First Printing August 2009

Library and Archives Canada Cataloguing in Publication
Learn to quilt with panels.
(Company's Coming crafts)
Includes index.
ISBN 978-1-897477-22-9
1. Quilting. 2. Quilting--Patterns I. Title: Quilt with panels. II. Series: Company's Coming crafts
TT835.L42 2009   746.46   C2008-908121-8

Published by
Company's Coming Publishing Limited
2311-96 Street
Edmonton, Alberta, Canada T6N 1G3
Tel: 780-450-6223 Fax: 780-450-1857
www.companyscoming.com

Company's Coming is a registered trademark owned by Company's Coming Publishing Limited

Printed in China

The Company's Coming Story

Jean Paré grew up with an understanding that family, friends and home cooking are the key ingredients for a good life. A mother of four, Jean worked as a professional caterer for 18 years, operating out of her home kitchen. During that time, she came to appreciate quick and easy recipes that call for everyday ingredients. In answer to mounting requests for her recipes, Company's Coming cookbooks were born, and Jean moved on to a new chapter in her career.

Company's Coming founder Jean Paré

Just as Company's Coming continues to promote the tradition of home cooking, the same is now true with crafting. Like good cooking, great craft results depend upon easy-to-follow instructions, readily available materials and enticing photographs of the finished products. Also, like cooking, crafting is meant to be enjoyed in the home or cottage. Company's Coming Crafts, then, is a natural extension from the kitchen into the family room or den.

In the beginning, Jean worked from a spare bedroom in her home, located in the small prairie town of Vermilion, Alberta, Canada. The first Company's Coming cookbook, *150 Delicious Squares*, was an immediate bestseller. Today, with well over 150 titles in print, Company's Coming has earned the distinction of publishing Canada's most popular cookbooks. The company continues to gain new supporters by adhering to Jean's "Golden Rule of Cooking"—Never share a recipe you wouldn't use yourself. It's an approach that has worked—millions of times over!

Company's Coming cookbooks are distributed throughout Canada, the United States, Australia and other international English-language markets. French- and Spanish-language editions have also been published. Sales to date have surpassed 25 million copies with no end in sight. Familiar and trusted in home kitchens around the world, Company's Coming cookbooks are highly regarded both as kitchen workbooks and as family heirlooms.

Because Company's Coming operates a test kitchen and not a craft shop, we've partnered with a major North American craft content publisher to assemble a variety of craft compilations exclusively for us. Our editors have been involved every step of the way. You can see the excellent results for yourself in the book you're holding.

Company's Coming Crafts are for everyone—whether you're a beginner or a seasoned pro. What better gift could you offer than something you've made yourself? In these hectic days, people still enjoy crafting parties; they bring family and friends together in the same way a good meal does. Company's Coming is proud to support crafters with this new creative book series.

We hope you enjoy these easy-to-follow, informative and colourful books, and that they inspire your creativity. So, don't delay—get crafty!

TABLE OF CONTENTS

Feeling Crafty? Get Creative! 6 • Foreword 7 • Quilting Basics 8

Pillow Panels:
General Instructions
Stitch up a quick table topper, placemat, wall quilt or throw using a pillow panel as the focus.

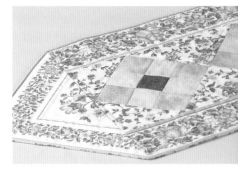

Square-Set Table Runner, page 20

Wake-Up Call, page 33

Off to Paris, page 28

Corner Cabins, page 24

TABLE OF CONTENTS

Cheater-Quilt Panels: General Instructions

Change a cheater-quilt panel into a one-of-a-kind quilt using your creativity and designs in this chapter.

Combination Panels: General Instructions

Create a fun quilt for any size bed in no time starting with a unique combination panel.

All My Friends, page 107

SS Rainbow, page 62

Hexagon Fancy, page 59

Feeling Crafty? Get Creative!

Each 160-page book features easy-to-follow, step-by-step instructions and full-page colour photographs of every project. Whatever your crafting fancy, there's a Company's Coming Creative Series craft book to match!

Beading: Beautiful Accessories in Under an Hour

Complement your wardrobe, give your home extra flair or add an extra-special personal touch to gifts with these quick and easy beading projects. Create any one of these special crafts in an hour or less.

Knitting: Easy Fun for Everyone

Take a couple of needles and some yarn and see what beautiful things you can make! Learn how to make fashionable sweaters, comfy knitted blankets, scarves, bags and other knitted crafts with these easy to intermediate knitting patterns.

Card Making: Handmade Greetings for All Occasions

Making your own cards is a fun, creative and inexpensive way of letting someone know you care. Stamp, emboss, quill or layer designs in a creative and unique card with your own personal message for friends or family.

Patchwork Quilting

In this book full of throws, baby quilts, table toppers, wall hangings—and more—you'll find plenty of beautiful projects to try. With the modern fabrics available, and the many practical and decorative applications, patchwork quilting is not just for Grandma!

Crocheting: Easy Blankets, Throws & Wraps

Find projects perfect for decorating your home, for looking great while staying warm or for giving that one-of-a-kind gift. A range of simple but stunning designs make crocheting quick, easy and entertaining.

Sewing: Fun Weekend Projects

Find a wide assortment of easy and attractive projects to help you create practical storage solutions, decorations for any room or just the right gift for that someone special. Create table runners, placemats, baby quilts, pillows and more!

For more information about Company's Coming craft books, visit our website, www.companyscoming.com

FOREWORD

Browsing through your local fabric store, you may have come across some beautiful printed panels but could not think of what you might do with them. Throughout this book, you will find lots of ideas and designs. Making quilts and quilted projects using preprint pillow panels, cheater panels and a combination of both is fun and exciting. Quilts work up quickly when large elements of preprint panels are used. You will be able to make a myriad of projects in all sizes and shapes.

You will probably not be able to find the exact panels used in the projects in this book, but you will find other great panels that will work with the designs given. We've included information on the different types of panels and how they can be used. Tips are also given on how to cut and adjust the size of the new panels you find. Once you choose your panel, you'll have fun finding coordinating fabrics in your stash or at your local store.

Pillow panels are a great place to start. Despite their name, you can create projects of all sizes from runners to bed quilts. For some designs, the panel can become the focus of a wall quilt with borders, sashing or pieced blocks providing an interesting frame. In other designs the main motif can be removed from the panel and appliquéd onto a project. Your pillow panel can become the focus for smaller projects like tote bags, table runners and toppers. The panel can also be cut in sections and pieced into a totally new design. The possibilities are endless.

You will also find cheater-quilt panels in all sizes which are intended to be used to make quick quilts. Using the designs in this book and your creativity, you can also turn one of these panels into a unique wall quilt or a medallion-style bed quilt. Stitch a cute baby quilt starting with a panel, adding matching bumper pads or other accessories for a delightful nursery set.

Combination panels are made up of many different motifs, either in same-size sections or random sizes. Many of these individual sections can be cut apart or specific motifs can be fussy-cut to create wonderful new designs for truly unique quilted projects. We've included several designs to get you started.

It's time for you to have fun creating wonderful quilted projects using panels. You'll be surprised at how quick and easy it can be!

Square-Set Table Runner, page 20

QUILTING BASICS

The Fabric

The preferred fabric for quiltmaking is 100 per cent cotton fabric. It is easy to work with and will wear much better than almost any other type of fabric.

Prewashing is not necessary, but pretesting your fabric for colourfastness and shrinkage is strongly advised. Start by cutting 2"-wide strips from each fabric that you will be using. To determine whether the fabric is colourfast, immerse each strip separately into a clean bowl of extremely hot water, or hold the fabric strip under hot running water. If your fabric bleeds a great deal, all is not lost. You might be able to wash all of that fabric until the excess dye has washed out. Fabrics that continue to bleed after they have been washed several times should not be used.

To test for shrinkage, take each saturated strip and iron it dry with a hot iron, being careful not to stretch it. When the strip is completely dry, measure and compare it to your original 2"-wide strip. If all your fabric strips shrink about the same amount, then you really have no problem. When you wash your finished quilt, you may achieve the puckered look of an antique quilt. If you do not want this look, you will have to wash and dry all of the fabric before beginning so that shrinkage is no longer a problem. Use spray starch or sizing when ironing fabric to give it a crisp finish.

Rotary Cutting

Supplies

For rotary cutting, you will need a mat, acrylic ruler and a rotary cutter. There are many different brands and types of supplies on the market. Choose one that is comfortable for you.

Mats come in various sizes, but if you are new to rotary cutting, an 18" x 24" mat is a good choice. Be sure to keep your mat on a flat surface when not in use so that it doesn't bend. Also, avoid storing it in direct sunlight—heat will cause the mat to become warped. Bent or warped mats will decrease the accuracy of your cutting.

Acrylic rulers are a must for safe and accurate cutting. Be sure your ruler has ⅛" increment markings in both directions as well as a 45-degree marking. Either the 6" x 24" or 6" x 12" size is recommended. The larger size is long enough to use with the fabric only folded once. Using the smaller size requires that you fold the fabric twice in order to cut.

There are several different rotary cutters currently available. Read the labels to find one with features that you prefer, such as type of handle, adaptability (for right- and left-handed use), safety, size and cost.

Cutting Strips

Iron fabric to remove wrinkles. Fold in half lengthwise, bringing selvages together. Fold in half again (Figure 1). Be sure there aren't any wrinkles in the fabric.

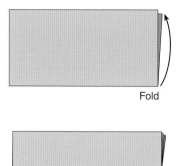

Fold

Fold again

Figure 1

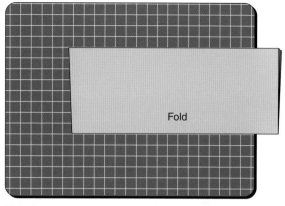

Fold

Right-handed

Square up fabric first. Place folded fabric on cutting mat with the fabric length on the right or left for left-handers (Figure 2). Line up fold of fabric along one of the mat grid lines.

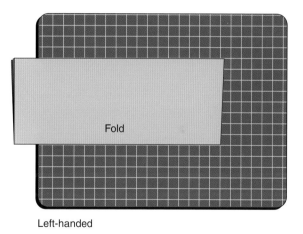

Fold

Left-handed

Figure 2

Place acrylic ruler near cut edge, with ruler markings even with mat grid. Hold ruler firmly with left hand (right hand for left-handers), with small finger off the mat to provide extra stability. Hold rotary cutter with blade against ruler and cut away from you in one motion (Figure 3).

Place ruler with appropriate width line along cut edge of fabric and cut strip (Figure 4). Continue cutting the number of strips needed for your project.

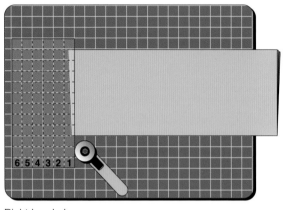

Right-handed

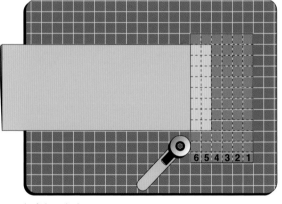

Right-handed

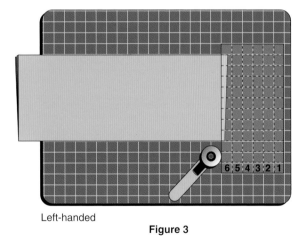

Left-handed

Figure 3

Left-handed

Note: *After cutting a few strips, check to make sure your fabric is squared up and re-square if necessary. If you don't, your strips may have a "v" in the centre (Figure 5), causing inaccurate piecing.*

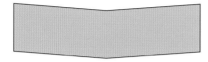

Figure 5

Strip Piecing
Strip piecing is a simple technique that can be used to achieve intricate effects.

The simplest form of strip piecing is sewing two different strips together (Figure 6).

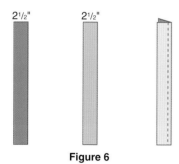

Figure 6

Press seam to one side, preferably toward the darker fabric (Figure 7).

Figure 7

To achieve squares in your finished block or border, cut the sewn strips in increments equaling the original cut width of the strips. For example, if you started with 2½"-wide strips, cut the sewn strips in 2½"-wide increments (Figure 8).

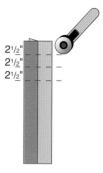

Figure 8

The cut segments can be sewn together in pairs to make a Four Patch (Figure 9), or sew more together to make a border (Figure 10).

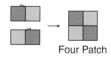

Four Patch

Figure 9

Figure 10

You can also sew three or more strips together in different arrangements for even more interesting results (Figure 11).

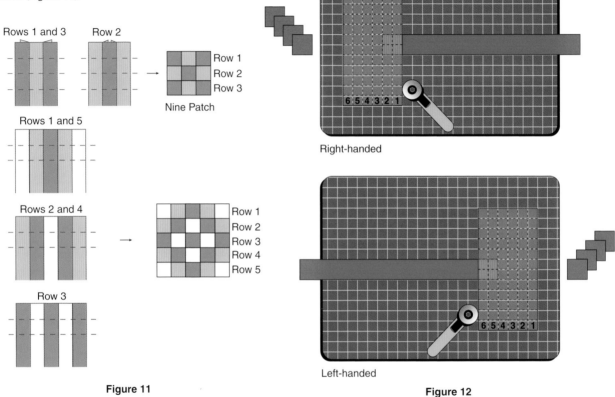

Right-handed

Left-handed

Figure 11

Figure 12

Cutting Squares and Rectangles

Place a stack of strips (no more than four) on cutting mat; be sure strips are lined up evenly. Cut required number of squares or rectangles referring to the project instructions (Figure 12).

Half-Square Triangles

Some of the blocks require half-square triangles. Half-square triangles have their short sides on the straight grain of the fabric. This is necessary if these edges are on the outer edge of the block.

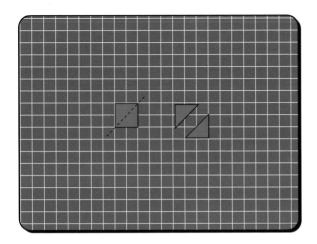

Figure 13

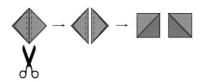

Figure 17

There are two ways to sew half-square triangles. First, cut squares the required size, then cut in half diagonally (Figure 13). Sew triangles together to form a square (Figure 14).

The second method is especially useful when many of the same triangle squares are needed for your project.

Note: If you will be sewing two squares together, place the strips for those squares right sides together, then cut into squares. Your squares will then be ready to sew together.

Figure 14

Press the strips together to allow strips to adhere slightly to one another for easier handling.

Second, cut squares the required size. Place two squares right sides together. Draw a diagonal line from corner to corner on wrong side of lighter square (Figure 15).

Finishing Your Quilt

Sandwich the batting between the completed top and prepared backing; pin or baste layers together to hold. *Note: If using basting spray to hold layers together, refer to instructions on the product container for use.*

Figure 15   **Figure 16**

Quilt as desired by hand or machine; remove pins or basting. Trim excess backing and batting even with quilt top.

Sew ¼" from each side of diagonal line (Figure 16).

Cut along drawn line to get two squares (Figure 17).

Join binding strips on short ends to make one long strip. Fold the strip in half along length with wrong sides together; press.

Sew binding to quilt edges, mitering corners and overlapping ends. Fold binding to the back side and stitch in place to finish.

PILLOW PANELS

Pillow panels have long been favourites of fabric companies.

These pretty panels feature many different designs from cute to elegant (Photos 1a and 1b). Although they are called pillow panels, they can be used for many other projects ranging in size from small to large. In this chapter we have shared some ideas for using pillow panels to create a number of interesting projects.

Photos 1a and 1b. Pillow panels feature many different designs.

Some of the projects in this chapter are examples of directional pillow panels being used as the focus of wall quilts. These include Ship Ahoy (page 44) and Off to Paris (page 28).

Other projects are examples of quick, decorative and useful items that start with a pillow panel as the focus or design idea. These include Wake-Up Call (page 33), Chenille Leopards (page 36) and Square-Set Table Runner (page 20).

The last grouping of projects shows ways to cut up and reuse panels in creative ways. Projects in this section include Going in Circles (page 40) and Corner Cabins (page 24).

One important thing to remember is that you probably won't find pillow panels exactly like those used in the book. Fabric companies manufacture new fabric lines every six months. The projects we share call for a certain type of pillow panel. Any panel of that type will work for the design.

What Is a Pillow Panel?

We are defining pillow panels as squares that are created by fabric companies with the idea that they will be used to make approximate 16"-square pillows.

Two panels, printed across the width, are included in a ½ yard of fabric. The two panels are usually coordinated but different (Photo 2). Most panel yardage includes an edge stripe along one or both selvage edges (Photo 3).

Photo 2. Two pillow panels are included in a ½ yard of fabric.

Photo 3. Border stripes are often on each selvage edge.

Some of our projects use only one design panel, but most use more than one. If two identical panels are needed, extra yardage is required.

Pillow Panel Types & Styles

There are two different types of pillow panels—directional and nondirectional.

Directional panels include designs that must be used in an upright position such as a vase of flowers or an animal panel (Photos 4a and 4b).

Photos 4a and 4b. A directional pillow panel has a top and bottom.

Nondirectional panels include designs with no specific top or bottom. These panels can be used in any direction (Photo 5).

Pillow panel styles include realistic designs such as animals, scenes, kids' motifs and florals (Photo 6).

Photo 5. This shows an example of a nondirectional panel.

Geometric panel styles include quilt designs, abstract motifs, circular designs and framed centres (Photo 7).

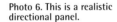

Photo 6. This is a realistic directional panel.

Photo 7. This is a geometric nondirectional panel.

The type and style of the panel often dictates its use. For example, a pillow panel with a directional kids' motif would not be appropriate to use as the focus of a king-size bed quilt made for an adult, just as a panel with a vase of flowers would not be interesting to a small child. Directional panel cannot be used in a project that sets the panel diagonally.

Problem-Solving When Using Pillow Panels

Purchase a complete panel. When purchasing the pillow panel yardage, be sure the fabric cutter opens the fabric and cuts evenly between panels. In some cases, we have actually seen the fabric cut through two layers and the underneath panel destroyed.

The pillow panel is not square. Often pillow panel designs that are intended to be square are not. They might be 1/16"–1/4" off, meaning that the panel could measure 16" on the sides and 16⅛" on the top and bottom. To use a panel in a project, it should be square.

To square up a pillow panel, select the size you want the panel to be. Decide what part of the design you want to preserve for use. You may have to add a little more to some sides when cutting to make square (Photo 8). Remember to include a ¼" seam allowance when cutting, but not when auditioning the panel for use.

Photo 8. Cutting beyond a design line is sometimes necessary to square the panel.

Photo 9. This panel has corners that are not square.

Another way a pillow panel might not be square is that the fabric is printed off-grain. That would mean that the panel corners are not square even when cut on a specific line on the panel (Photo 9). Sometimes this problem can be solved with pressing.

Use a hot iron with steam or a spray water bottle. Hold on to the panel at the corner that needs to be squared. Pull

in the direction it needs to go to be square, pressing with the steam iron. You can also press after having sprayed the square to dampen. (Photo 10). The steam combined with the pulling action moves the threads and helps to stretch the fabric back into a square position.

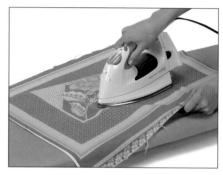

Photo 10. Pull on panel corners while ironing with steam to square up a corner.

The design area is not printed to a specific size. We found that it is common for pillow panels to be printed in very strange sizes. It is rare to find a panel with an exact measurement such as a 16" square. Many panels are sized in strange increments such as a 15⅞" square.

A solution to this is to cut into the separating area between the panels to add size. Be careful when cutting, though, because if this space is not exactly perpendicular to the panel outline, the space will appear to be uneven when stitching later. Sometimes it is impossible for this space to be exactly the same from one end of the piece to another; for example, if the panel is not square and you are cutting to make it square (Photo 11). Don't worry too much about this as it rarely makes a difference in the finished project (Photo 12).

Photo 11. Sometimes it is not possible to cut along a printed line along the edge of the entire panel.

Photo 12. This project was not cut along one printed straight line on the panel.

Edge stripe is too short to be useful. If purchasing a ½ yard of pillow panel fabric, you will end up with 1 yard of stripe if each side of the panel fabric has a stripe (Photo 13). This yardage is not enough to surround even one panel.

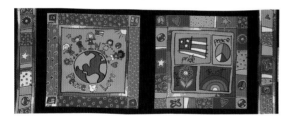

Photo 13. Stripe on both sides of the panel can be used in creative ways.

If you like the stripe, save it to be cut up and used in smaller pieces in the project, or use the stripe in other projects as in the Square-Set Table Runner (page 20).

The panel is difficult to cut on a specific line. Many pillow panels include at least one solid line around the design motif. As previously discussed, when panels are not square, it is difficult to cut them on a specific line as the result will also not be square. Stretching while pressing

helps, but if the lines are not printed accurately, even perfectly square corners won't yield squared lines.

Choose a line on the pillow panel that you would like to be the stitching line. Measure from that line to the opposite side of the panel to the same design line and remember the measurement (Photo 14). Repeat on the two remaining sides of the panel. If the measurements are the same, you are all set to cut. If not, you will have to cut the inaccurate side to the same size as the perfect side. This means that the finished project will not look exactly the same on all sides of the panel. In most cases, this is not a problem. Accurate cutting and stitching is more important than accurate printed lines.

Photo 14. Measure to the same line on the opposite side.

Find coordinating fabrics. Some pillow panel designs have been planned with coordinating fabrics. Some fabric companies add a stripe and several prints of different values to the line to allow the consumer to plan projects that will have a specific look.

It is not necessary to use only fabrics from one collection— it can be interesting to add other fabrics in prints, solids and tone-on-tones. Don't feel that you have to use only the fabrics the manufacturer created to match the panels.

Ways to Use Pillow Panels

There are many ways to use pillow panels. We have tried to share as many as space permits, but had many more design ideas than could fit in one book.

Set the panel in a different way. Pillow panels can be set straight or on point depending on the directional qualities.

Use a panel as the focus of a wall quilt. With so many different motifs available, a pillow panel can be used as the centre focus of a medallion-style project. Borders, sashing and pieced or appliquéd blocks can be added all around to increase to a larger size.

Use a motif from panel in a small decorative or useful item. The main motif of a pillow panel can be removed from the panel and appliquéd or pieced into a project. Wake-Up Call (page 33) uses the rooster design from a panel as the focus of a placemat. This is a very simple way to use some of the beautiful motifs that are often found in pillow panels (Photo 15).

Photo 15. Isolate a design to cut and fuse, and use as the focus of a project.

Use a pillow panel as the design focus for a small project. Tote bags, table runners or toppers are the perfect places to feature one or two pillow panels. The Square-Set Table Runner (page 20) uses one panel as the design focus. Any panel may be used to create this project.

Cut a pillow panel in sections. Nondirectional, geometric panels may be cut in sections and reused to create interesting projects. The centre of a pillow panel can be used as one block, and the cut-off corners can be used as another block in a wall quilt (Photo 16). This type of project is fun to stitch because it works up quickly and does not resemble the original panel when complete.

Photo 16. The corners were removed from this panel and reused to create a second block design.

Keep design size and design placement consistent. Borders or other design elements within the squares can be inconsistent in size from square to square. If this is true of your panel, it is difficult, but not impossible, to use the panel. Choose a project that uses just one panel, or in which the panel is bordered. Then the size can be enlarged or made smaller without the inconsistency interfering with the quality of the finished project.

Making a Pillow Panel Fit the Project

If you find you want to create a project that requires a specific size pillow panel and your panel is not the right size, you have several options.

Enlarge the size of the pillow panel. To enlarge the size of the panel, you have two options. The first includes cutting into the separating area between panels as shown in Photo 17. This option is easy, as the background is usually perfectly coordinated with elements from the panel.

Photo 17. Use the separating area to enlarge a panel.

The second option for enlarging is to add border strips all around. This can be done to alternate sides with butted strips or with mitred corners. Cut oversized strips and trim after stitching to create the desired-size panel needed with seams. For example, if you have a 12"-square pillow panel and your design requires a 14"-square pillow panel, you need to add 2" to the size. That means that you need a 1" strip all around. To be safe, cut the strips 3" wide and trim after stitching to 14½" x 14½" (Photo 18). This will also solve any problems you might have with the panel not being square.

Photo 18. Add wider strips than necessary and trim to size.

Reduce the size of the pillow panel. To reduce the size of the panel, cut away equal amounts of panel sections around the centre motif. Be sure the centre motif remains centred in your trimmed panel (Photo 19). This may not be an appropriate strategy for all panels. Be sure the required panel size is at least as large as the panel motif to avoid destroying the design.

Photo 19. Cut away design elements to reduce the size of a panel.

Protect the outer pillow panel elements. Anything trimmed away can be used in the current project or in future projects. Try not to cut into the areas around the panel unless necessary. Choose a way to cut all the separating elements and save them to use as block borders or in pieced areas (Photo 20). ■

Photo 20. Do not destroy surrounding areas when cutting panels.

SQUARE-SET TABLE RUNNER

Use a pillow panel to make a table runner so fast you'll want a new one for every month of the year!

Design | Sandra L. Hatch & Sue Harvey

Project Specifications
Skill Level: Beginner
Runner Size: 57" x 15½"
Panel Size: 15½" x 15½"

Materials
One 2" x 10" strip green tonal
Two 2¼" x 10" strips blue mottled
One 2" x 21" strip blue mottled
Two 2¼" x 21" strips pink mottled
⅓ yard floral print
1 yard pillow panel
Backing 59" x 18"
Batting 59" x 18"
Neutral colour all-purpose thread
Clear nylon monofilament
Basting spray
Basic sewing tools and supplies

Project Notes
Begin with a ½-yard pillow panel piece that includes two panels across the width. One panel is used as the centre. Use the remaining panel as the runner's end triangles. Use portions of the panel edge stripe in the pieced sections. This makes good use of the entire yardage.

Look for a panel that is nondirectional for the diagonal setting to avoid placing the motif on its side (Photo 1). This eliminates most scenic and animal panels. Any panel can be used for the square setting. However, if your table will be used from both sides, the motif will be upside down when viewed from one side or the other (Photo 2).

Photo 1. Look for a nondirectional panel for a diagonal setting.

Photo 2. A directional panel will be upside down on one side of the table.

Also consider the outer corners of the panel when making a selection. An approximate 10" square corner from opposite sides of the panel will be used as the end

triangles on your runner (Photo 3). Choose a panel with corners that will be attractive when cut to this size. Avoid panels that will leave only an unrecognizable or awkward portion of the motif in the corner (Photo 4).

Photo 3. A 10"-square corner will be used as end triangles.

Photo 4. Avoid panels with corners that do not work for the end triangles.

The sample project used panels that include a distinct border on the outer edge of the square. The panel edge stripe used on the pieced section is different than that on the end triangle, so it would not match on both the inside and outside lines regardless of how it was cut. We chose to match the outside lines to make a continuous outside edge (Photo 5). If you prefer to evenly match the end triangles to the pieced sections, choose a panel without a distinct outline.

Photo 5. The outside lines of the end triangle and pieced section match to make a continuous line.

The sample runner uses edge stripe from 1 yard of panel fabric. The two unused panels in the yardage could be hemmed for use as coordinating napkins, or backed and stuffed with fibrefill to use as chair-seat or -back cushions for an easy set.

Piecing the Top

Sew the 21" blue mottled strip between the two pink mottled strips with right sides together along length to make an A strip set as shown in Figure 1; press seams toward pink strips. Cut into eight 2¼" A segments, again referring to Figure 1.

Figure 1

Sew the green tonal strip between the two 10" blue mottled strips with right sides together along length to make a B strip set as shown in Figure 2; press seams toward green strip. Cut into four 2" B segments, again referring to Figure 2.

Figure 2

Sew a B segment between two A segments to complete an A-B unit as shown in Figure 3; press seams toward the A segments. Repeat for four A-B units.

Figure 3

Cut one 8⅜" x 8⅜" square floral print; cut the square on both diagonals to make four C triangles.

Cut four 4½" x 4½" squares floral print; cut each square on one diagonal to make eight D triangles.

Join two A-B units with two C triangles and four D triangles in diagonal rows as shown in Figure 4; join the rows to complete one A-B-C-D unit. Repeat for two units. Trim to measure 7⅛" x 14¾", if necessary.

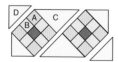

Figure 4

Cut four 3½" x 14¾" strips from the panel edge stripe, centring the stripe in the 3½" width. Sew a strip to opposite long sides of each pieced unit to complete the end sections; press seams toward strips.

Cut one 16" x 16" panel square, centring the panel motif in the square. *Note: If your panel does not fit within a 15½"-finished square area, refer to Making a Pillow Panel Fit the Project on page 18 for hints about changing the size of the square.*

Centre and sew an end section to opposite sides of the panel square; press seams toward the end section.

Choose the corners of one remaining panel to be used for the end triangles. Cut out the panel square, leaving ¼" beyond its edge. Measure 10⅛" from one corner along adjacent sides and make a mark as shown in Figure 5. Draw a line between marks; cut along the marked line as shown in Figure 6. Repeat on the opposite corner for two triangles. *Note: If your panel corner and edge stripe have outlines to be matched on their outside edges, trim the panel square ¼" from the outline before marking to cut the triangle as shown in Figure 7.*

Sew a triangle to each end of the pieced runner to complete the top as shown in Figure 8; press seams toward the triangles.

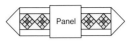

Figure 8

Completing the Runner

Apply basting spray to one side of the batting; place the wrong side of the completed top on the sprayed side and smooth. Trim batting even with the top.

Place the backing piece right sides together with the top; pin to hold. Trim the backing even with the top and batting.

Stitch all around, leaving a 6" opening on one edge of the A–B–C section.

Clip inverted angles and trim points. Turn right side out through the opening; hand-stitch the opening closed. Press edges flat.

Machine-quilt as desired and ¼" from the outer edges using clear nylon monofilament in the top of the machine and all-purpose thread in the bobbin. ∎

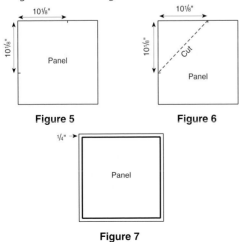

Figure 5   **Figure 6**

Figure 7

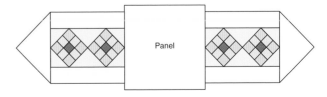

Square-Set Table Runner
Placement Diagram
57" x 15½"

CORNER CABINS

Add Log Cabin triangles to set off Baltimore Album–style preprint squares in this striking quilt.

Design | Sue Harvey

Project Specifications

Skill Level: Beginner
Quilt Size: 55½" x 70"
Block Size: 14½" x 14½"
Number of Blocks: 12

Materials

(12) 10¾" x 10¾" preprint squares
⅜ yard gold print
⅔ yard pink print
⅞ yard cream mottled
⅞ yard burgundy print
2⅛ yards green print
Backing 62" x 76"
Batting 62" x 76"
All-purpose thread to match fabrics
Hand- or machine-quilting thread
Basic sewing tools and supplies

Corner Cabins
14½" x 14½" Block

Project Note

The preprint squares used in this project are placed diagonally in the quilt. Look for squares with motifs that are not directional.

Cutting

Cut three 3⅝" by fabric width strips cream mottled; subcut into (24) 3⅝" squares. Cut each square on one diagonal to make 48 A triangles.

Cut six 2½" by fabric width strips cream mottled; set aside for J and K borders.

Cut two 4½" by fabric width strips pink print; subcut into (48) 1" B segments.

Cut two 5" by fabric width strips pink print; subcut into (48) 1" C segments.

Cut two 5¾" by fabric width strips burgundy print; subcut into (48) 1¼" D segments.

Cut two 6½" by fabric width strips burgundy print; subcut into (48) 1¼" E segments.

Cut two 7½" by fabric width strips green print; subcut into (48) 1½" F segments.

Corner Cabins

Cut two 8½" by fabric width strips green print; subcut into (48) 1½" G segments.

Cut six 3½" by fabric width strips green print; set aside for L and M borders.

Cut seven 2¼" by fabric width strips green print; set aside for binding.

Cut six 1½" by fabric width strips gold print; set aside for H and I borders.

Corner Cabins
Placement Diagram
55½" x 70"

Completing Blocks

Sew B to one short edge of A, aligning one end of B with the square corner of A as shown in Figure 1. Press seam toward B; leave excess B extending beyond A.

Figure 1

Sew C to the remaining short edge of A, again referring to Figure 1; press seam toward C.

Add D–G to the A-B-C unit in alphabetical order as shown in Figure 2; press seams toward the last strip added.

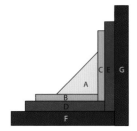

Figure 2

Trim the ends of the strips even with the edge of the A triangle as shown in Figure 3 to complete one Log Cabin triangle. Repeat to complete 48 triangles. *Note: Each triangle should measure 8⅛" on the F and G edges and 11½" on the A edge as shown in Figure 3.*

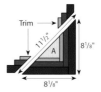

Figure 3

Sew a Log Cabin triangle to opposite sides of each preprint square as shown in Figure 4; press seams toward the square.

Figure 4

Sew a Log Cabin triangle to the remaining sides of each preprint square to complete the blocks, again referring to Figure 4; press seams toward the square.

Completing the Top

Join three blocks to make a row; press seams in one direction. Repeat for four rows.

Join the rows to complete the pieced centre; press seams in one direction.

Join the H-I strips on short ends to make a long strip; cut two 58½" H strips and two 46" I strips from the pieced strip.

Sew H to opposite long sides and I to the top and bottom of the pieced centre; press seams toward strips.

Join the J-K strips on short ends to make a long strip; cut two 60½" J strips and two 50" K strips from the pieced strip.

Sew J to opposite long sides and K to the top and bottom of the pieced centre; press seams toward strips.

Join the L-M strips on short ends to make a long strip; cut two 64½" L strips and two 56" M strips from the pieced strip.

Sew L to opposite long sides and M to the top and bottom of the pieced centre to complete the top; press seams toward strips.

Finishing the Quilt

Sandwich the batting between the completed top and prepared backing.

Hand- or machine-quilt as desired. When quilting is complete, trim batting and backing even with top.

Join the green print binding strips on short ends to make one long strip; press seams to one side. Fold the strip along length with wrong sides together; press.

Sew the binding strip to the quilt top, mitring corners and overlapping ends. Fold binding strip to the back; hand-stitch in place to finish. ■

OFF TO PARIS

Take a trip to Paris via the fabric trail in this colourful wall quilt.

Design | Sue Penn & Roxane Wright

Project Specifications
Skill Level: Beginner
Quilt Size: 44" x 44"

Materials
12½" x 12½" A panel (map of Paris)
¼ yard yellow tonal
⅓ yard each green, purple and aqua tonals
⅜ yard peach tonal
⅜ yard each green poodle and peach luggage prints
½ yard yellow umbrella print
1 yard coordinating stripe
Backing 50" x 50"
Batting 50" x 50"
Neutral colour all-purpose thread
Quilting thread
Basic sewing tools and supplies

Cutting
Cut one 2½" by fabric width strip each green (B), purple (C) and aqua (E) tonals.

Cut five 5¼" x 5¼" squares each purple (L), green (M), peach (N) and aqua (O) tonals. Cut each square on both diagonals to make 20 each L, M, N and O triangles.

Cut four 4½" x 4½" F squares peach tonal.

Cut two 2½" by fabric width D strips yellow tonal; subcut one strip into eight 2½" D squares.

Cut four 2½" x 20½" G strips and four 2½" x 32½" J strips coordinating stripe.

Cut five 2¼" by fabric width strips coordinating stripe for binding.

Cut two 4½" by fabric width strips each peach luggage (H) and green poodle (I) prints; subcut strips into (14) 4½" squares each fabric.

Cut three 4½" by fabric width strips yellow umbrella print; subcut strips into (20) 4½" K squares.

Completing the Quilt
Sew the B strip to the C strip with right sides together along the length; press seam toward B.

Subcut the B-C strip set into (12) 2½" B-C units as shown in Figure 1.

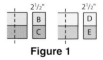

Figure 1

Sew the D strip to the E strip with right sides together along the length; press seam toward E.

Off to Paris

Subcut the D-E strip set into (12) 2½" D-E units, again referring to Figure 1.

Join three each B-C and D-E units to make a side strip as shown in Figure 2; press seams in one direction. Repeat to make four side strips.

Figure 2

Sew a side strip to opposite sides of A; press seams toward A.

Sew an F square to each end of the remaining side strips; press seams toward F.

Sew the F-side strip to the remaining sides of A to complete the pieced centre; press seams toward A.

Sew a G strip to opposite sides of the pieced centre; press seams toward G strips.

Sew a D square to each end of each remaining G strip; press seams toward G. Sew the D-G strips to the remaining sides of the pieced centre; press seams toward the D-G strips.

Join three each H and I squares to make an H-I side strip as shown in Figure 3; press seams in one direction. Repeat to make two strips. Sew an H-I strip to opposite sides of the pieced centre; press seams toward G strips.

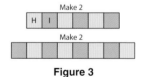

Figure 3

Join four each H and I squares to make longer H-I side strips, again referring to Figure 3; press seams in one direction. Repeat to make two longer H-I side strips. Sew these strips to the remaining sides of the pieced centre; press seams toward G strips.

Sew J to opposite sides of the pieced centre; press seams toward J strips.

Sew D to each end of each remaining J strip; press seams toward J. Sew a D-J strip to the remaining sides of the pieced centre; press seams toward the D-J strips.

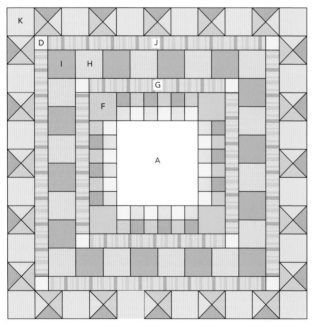

Off to Paris
Placement Diagram
44" x 44"

Sew L to M and N to O as shown in Figure 4; press seams toward L and N. Repeat to make 20 each L-M and N-O units.

Figure 4

Join one each L-M and N-O units to complete a triangle unit as shown in Figure 5; press seams in one direction. Repeat to make 20 triangle units.

Figure 5

Join four K squares and five triangle units to make a K strip as shown in Figure 6; press seams toward K. Repeat to make four K strips. Add K to each end of two strips; press seams toward K.

Figure 6

Sew the shorter K strips to opposite sides and longer K strips to the remaining sides of the pieced centre; press seams toward J strips to complete the pieced top.

Layer, quilt and bind referring to Finishing Your Quilt on page 13. ■

Wake-Up Call

WAKE-UP CALL

*Choose a pillow panel with a distinct
shape to cut out for appliqué.*

Design | Sandra L. Hatch & Sue Harvey

Project Specifications
Skill Level: Beginner
Placemat Size: 21" x 13"

Materials
1 pillow panel with large single motif
2 strips each 1½" by fabric width burgundy and blue
    tone-on-tones
15½" x 7½" rectangle cream check tone-on-tone
⅓ yard each tan and green tone-on-tones
Backing 24" x 16"
Batting 24" x 16"
Neutral colour all-purpose thread
Quilting thread
Clear nylon monofilament
⅓ yard fusible web
Basic sewing tools and supplies

Project Notes
Pillow panels have wonderful designs. Sometimes they
feature an animal or other realistic motifs. The rooster in
this panel makes the perfect design to cut out and fuse to
the background of this pieced placemat.

This same technique can be used to make other quilted
projects. Many designs could be used to create blocks for
a sampler bed-size quilt, or one design could be centred
to create a wall-size quilt.

Seasonal pillow-panel designs are abundant, making it
possible to make quick quilted projects for your home
that can be changed with the seasons.

Top Construction
Cut two strips green tone-on-tone and six strips tan
tone-on-tone 1½" by fabric width.

Photo 1. Here is an example of a rooster panel.

Sew a tan tone-on-tone strip between one each blue and burgundy tone-on-tone strip with right sides together along length to make an A strip set referring to Figure 1; repeat for two A strip sets. Press seams away from tan strips.

Figure 1

Sew a green tone-on-tone strip between two tan tone-on-tone strips with right sides together along length to make a B strip set, again referring to Figure 1; repeat for two B strip sets. Press seams toward green strips.

Subcut all strip sets into 1½" segments, again referring to Figure 1.

Join 10 B segments with 11 A segments, turning A segments to make a C border strip referring to Figure 2; repeat for two C border strips.

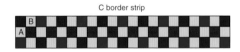

C border strip

Figure 2

Join four B segments with three A segments to make a D border strip, turning A segments as shown in Figure 3. Repeat for two D border strips.

D border strip

Figure 3

Sew a D border strip to opposite short ends of the 15½" x 7½" cream check tone-on-tone rectangle as shown in Figure 4; press seams away from D.

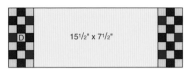

Figure 4

Sew a C border strip to opposite long sides of the pieced section as shown in Figure 5 to complete placemat base; press seams toward strips.

Figure 5

Appliqué

Bond the fusible web to the wrong side of the pillow panel motif. Cut out the shape following edges of motif; remove paper backing.

Position the motif on the left end of the finished base overlapping into the pieced borders referring to the Placement Diagram for positioning suggestions. When satisfied with placement, fuse in place following manufacturer's instructions.

Completing the Quilt

Sandwich batting between the completed top and prepared backing piece; pin or baste layers together to hold flat for quilting.

Using clear nylon monofilament in the top of the machine and all-purpose thread in the bobbin, straight-stitch around fused motif close to edges and around inside lines on the motif as desired.

Prepare for quilting and quilt as desired by hand or machine referring to page 13 for instructions.

Cut two 2¼" by fabric width strips green tone-on-tone for binding. Bind edges of quilt referring to page 13 to finish. ■

Wake-Up Call
Placement Diagram
21" x 13"

CHENILLE LEOPARDS

Any colourful pillow panel can be turned into an elegant 3-D pillow using this easy stitching method.

Design | Sandra L. Hatch & Sue Harvey

Project Specifications
Skill Level: Beginner
Pillow Size: 23½" x 23½"
Panel Size: 16" x 16"

Materials
4 identical pillow panels with border edging (2 yards)
¾ yard backing fabric
All-purpose thread to match fabric
14" x 14" pillow form
¼" or ⅜" chenille cutting strip
Basting spray
Basic sewing tools and supplies

Project Notes
Most pillow panels are printed with four panels in a yard with two different panels in each yard (Photo 1). The panels used to make the sample pillow are no exception (Photo 2). To make one chenille pillow, you need four identical panels. You may need to purchase 2 yards of panel fabric.

The panel yardage will probably have a related border print as shown in Photo 1. The sample pillow was made using a leopard-print panel. The border strip running along both edges was used to make the flange around the outside of the pillow.

Photo 1. Pillow panels usually include two different panels in a yard.

Photo 2. The panel shown is the second panel design included in the yardage for the sample project.

Instructions

Cut four identical pillow panels 16½" x 16½". *Note: Any size panel will work; cut to the same size and along the exact same edge so panels are identical.*

Draw a diagonal line from corner to corner on one panel. Subsequent sewing lines need not be marked if your sewing machine needle can be moved. Stitching lines on the sample are ⅜" apart, but you may prefer to stitch ½" apart.

Layer the panels and pin layers matching identical areas to align; spray-baste layers together to hold.

Stitch on the marked line from corner to corner as shown in Figure 1. Turn the panel and begin stitching the next line ⅜" or ½" away from the first line, referring to Figure 2. Continue sewing the same distance from the previously stitched line, turning the top to begin sewing at the previous seam end to avoid stretching all in one direction.

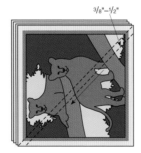

Figure 1 **Figure 2**

When the entire top has been stitched, slip the ¼" chenille cutting strip into the channel formed between stitches as shown in Figure 3. *Note: The top three layers are cut and*

the bottom layer is left intact. If your channel is ½" wide, use the ⅜" chenille cutting strip.

Figure 3

Using a rotary cutter, cut through the centre of the channel as shown in Figure 4; repeat for all channels.

Figure 4

Put your stitched panel in the washing machine with a load of towels; place in the dryer when washed.

After drying, trim away all frayed threads and brush your hand across the surface of the pillow top to smooth. The channels should be open and have a ruffled, ragged appearance. Rewash to make more ragged, if desired.

Cut four 4¼" x 24" strips border stripe. *Note: If your border stripe is wider or narrower, cut it any width. These instructions create the pillow as shown.*

Sew a border stripe strip to each side of the pillow panel, mitring corners. Trim mitred seam allowance to ¼" as shown in Figure 5; press seam open.

Figure 5

Cut two 14¼" x 24" backing pieces. Press under one 24" edge of each piece ¼"; press under ½". Stitch to hem edges.

Pin the backing pieces right sides together with the bordered pillow panel, overlapping the hemmed edges in the centre 3" as shown in Figure 6; baste along overlapped edges.

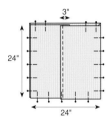

Figure 6

Stitch all around outside edge of layered pieces; turn right side out. Press edges flat.

Figure 7

Stitch ¼" from inside border seam allowance on pillow front to make flange as shown in Figure 7. Insert pillow form through back opening to finish. ■

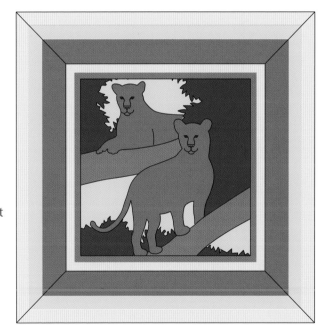

Chenille Leopards
Placement Diagram
23½" x 23½"

GOING IN CIRCLES

Make a beautiful faux Drunkard's Path quilt in a day using a pillow panel with a round, framed design.

Design | Sandra L. Hatch & Sue Harvey

Project Specifications
Skill Level: Beginner
Quilt Size: 45" x 45"
Panel Size: 12" x 12"

Materials
2½ yards round-design pillow panel with borders
   or 10 panels and 1 yard coordinating stripe
¼ yard coordinating print
⅜ yard coordinating mottled or solid
Backing 51" x 51"
Batting 51" x 51"
Neutral colour all-purpose thread
Quilting thread
Basic sewing tools and supplies

Project Notes
The pillow panel used to create this faux Drunkard's Path look must have a circular design in the centre. The sample used a panel with a Christmas design. Any nondirectional circular-design panel will work.

For this project, the frame section of each panel was removed to result in 12" x 12" squares (Photo 1). These squares were cut in quarters to make 6" x 6" squares.

Photo 1. Remove the frame.

The fabric yardage included a wide border stripe on the edges with narrow stripes separating the panels (Photo 2). Because of all these other designs printed in the yardage, the panel itself is smaller than many others, resulting in a small wall-size quilt.

Photo 2. The panel yardage has border stripe and separating strips.

Going in Circles

If your pillow panel yardage doesn't have the border stripe, your quilt will be larger with longer border strips. This will require the purchase of several yards of coordinating border fabric or stripe.

More rows may be added, but the design works best when the centre of the quilt is square.

Alternate layouts are possible with this simple design. We have shown two possibilities to help you create this quick-and-easy quilt in Figure 3 (page 43).

Instructions

Separate pillow panels into equal-size squares, removing any frame section from each panel. *Note: The sample yielded 12" squares after removing frames. If you remove the frame section carefully, it can be saved for future use in other projects.*

Cut nine panels through the centre to make four separate units from each panel as shown in Figure 1.

Figure 1

Arrange the cut square sections in six rows of six squares each referring to Figure 2; join squares in rows. Press seams in one direction. Join the rows to complete the pieced centre; press seams in one direction.

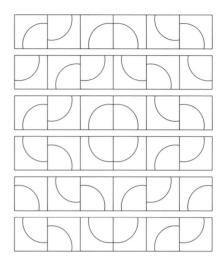

Figure 2

Cut two 1½" x 33½" A strips and two 1½" x 35½" B strips coordinating print. Sew B to opposite sides and A to the top and bottom of the pieced centre; press seams toward strips. *Note: If your panel squares are larger or smaller than 12" x 12", measure your quilt and adjust border lengths.*

Cut four 5½" x 35½" D strips coordinating strip or border. Sew a D strip to opposite sides; press seams toward strips.

Cut four 5½" x 5½" E squares from the remaining pillow panel, cutting identical parts of the panel for each square.

Sew an E square to each end of the remaining D strips, positioning squares with motif edges toward the quilt centre referring to the Placement Diagram of the quilt; press seams toward D.

Sew the D-E strips to the top and bottom of the pieced centre; press seams toward strips.

Prepare for quilting and quilt as desired by hand or machine referring to page 13 for instructions.

Cut five 2¼" by fabric width strips coordinating mottled or solid for binding. Bind edges of quilt referring to page 13 to finish. ■

Photo 3. A non-holiday wreath was used here in the same design.

Going in Circles
Placement Diagram
45" x 45"

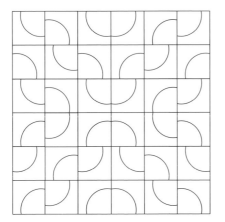

Figure 3

SHIP AHOY

*A scenic pillow panel creates the
focal point of a quick wall quilt.*

Design | Sandra L. Hatch & Sue Harvey

Project Specifications
Skill Level: Intermediate
Quilt Size: 38" x 38"
Panel Size: 16" x 16"

Materials
⅜ yard gold print
¾ yard each red, cream and blue prints
½ yard pillow panel
Backing 44" x 44"
Batting 44" x 44"
Neutral colour all-purpose thread
Quilting thread
Basic sewing tools and supplies

Project Notes
The pieced border of this pattern can be used with any
pillow panel centre. The sample project includes one
coordinating fabric that is part of the same fabric line
as the panel. Using at least one same-line fabric gives a
more planned look to the project, especially when using a
panel with a distinctive motif like the nautical-theme in
the sample.

Pillow panel yardage usually includes a border stripe on
each edge of the fabric. The border stripe on the pillow
panel used for this project included small separate motifs
that complement the panel (Photo 1). These motifs were
easily isolated and fussy-cut as 3½" squares to use in the
pieced border Four-Patch corners (Photo 2 on page 46).

Photo 1. The border stripe includes small separate motifs.

Lighthouse panel used for this project.

Ship Ahoy

Photo 2. Separate motifs may be fussy-cut.

Cutting

Cut six 1½" by fabric width strips red print; subcut into two strips each 1½" x 16½" for A, 1½" x 18½" for B, 1½" x 30½" for C and 1½" x 32½" for D.

Cut one 3½" by fabric width strip red print; subcut into eight 3½" E squares.

Cut four 2¼" by fabric width strips red print; set aside for binding.

Cut two strips 4¼" by fabric width cream print; subcut into (10) 4¼" squares. Cut each square on both diagonals to make 40 cream F triangles as shown in Figure 1. Cut one strip 2⅜" by fabric width cream print; subcut into eight 2⅜" squares. Cut each square on one diagonal to make 16 G triangles, again referring to Figure 1.

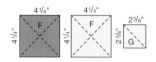

Figure 1

Cut five strips 2" by fabric width cream print; subcut into (96) 2" H squares.

Cut two strips 4¼" by fabric width blue print; subcut into (12) 4¼" squares. Cut each square on both diagonals to make 48 blue F triangles, again referring to Figure 1.

Cut two strips each blue print 3½" x 32½" for J and 3½" x 38½" for K; set aside for borders.

Cut three 3½" by fabric width strips gold print; subcut into (48) 2" x 3½" I rectangles.

Cut one 16½" x 16½" square from pillow panel yardage, centring the panel motif in the square. *Note: The sample panel design measures only 14½" x 14½". This design was centred in the 16½" square needed, and the additional width and length was cut from the fabric surrounding the panel motif. This made a 1" (¾"-finished) border around the motif.*

Cut eight 3½" x 3½" squares from pillow panel border stripe, referring to the Project Notes for cutting suggestions.

Piecing Borders

Draw a diagonal line from corner to corner on the wrong side of each H square.

Place an H square right sides together with I as shown in Figure 2; stitch on the marked line, trim the seam allowance to ¼" and press H open, again referring to Figure 2.

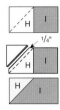

Figure 2

Repeat on the remaining end of I to complete one H-I unit as shown in Figure 3; repeat to make 48 H-I units.

Figure 3

Join 12 H-I units to make a strip as shown in Figure 4; press seams in one direction. Repeat for four H-I strips.

Figure 4

Join five cream F triangles with six blue F triangles to make a strip as shown in Figure 5; press seams in one direction.

Figure 5

Add a G triangle to each end to complete one F-G strip, again referring to Figure 5; press seams toward G. Repeat for eight F-G strips.

Sew an F-G strip to opposite sides of an H-I strip to make a pieced border strip as shown in Figure 6; press seams toward the F-G strips. Repeat for four pieced border strips.

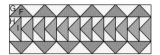

Figure 6

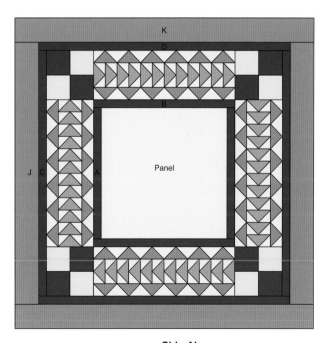

Ship Ahoy
Placement Diagram
38" x 38"

Join two E squares with two border stripe squares to make a Four-Patch unit as shown in Figure 7; repeat for four Four-Patch units. *Note: The sample border stripe has directional motifs. In this case, the Four-Patch units must be made to place the motifs upright as shown in Figure 8. If your border stripe motif is not directional, the Four-Patch units may be turned for positioning in the border corners and all made as shown in Figure 7.*

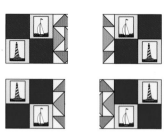

Figure 9

Figure 7

Make 2   Make 2

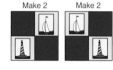

Figure 8

Completing the Quilt

Sew an A strip to opposite sides of the panel square and a B strip to the top and bottom; press seams toward strips.

Sew a pieced border strip to opposite sides of the centre referring to the Placement Diagram for positioning of strips; press seams toward the A strips.

Sew a Four-Patch unit to each end of the remaining pieced border strips referring to the Placement Diagram for positioning of the units. *Note: For directional motifs, position Four-Patch units as shown in Figure 9.*

Sew the strips to the top and bottom of the centre referring to the Placement Diagram for positioning of strips; press seams toward B strips.

Sew a C strip to opposite sides of the centre and a D strip to the top and bottom; press seams toward strips.

Sew a J strip to opposite sides of the centre and a K strip to the top and bottom; press seams toward strips to complete the top.

Prepare for quilting and quilt as desired by hand or machine referring to page 13 for instructions.

Bind edges of quilt using the previously cut red print binding strips referring to page 13 to finish. ■

CHEATER-QUILT PANELS

Cheater-quilt panels are intended to be batted, backed, quilted or tied, and bound to make a quilt just as they are purchased.

There are several types of cheater-quilt panels. We have used examples of each in the projects in this chapter.

Cheater-quilt panels are available in typical sizes—wall-quilt panels, crib-quilt panels, lap-quilt panels and bed-quilt yardage.

Wall-, crib- and lap-quilt panels share similarities in preparation and use methods. Wall-quilt panels are used to make wall quilts; crib-quilt panels are used to make crib quilts; and lap-quilt panels are used to make lap quilts. Bed-quilt yardage is used to make larger-size bed quilts. Sometimes it is printed 90" in order to make quilting larger-size quilts easier.

But in this chapter, we have thrown out the intended use of the cheater-quilt panels and demonstrated how you can create something entirely different.

Wall-Quilt Panels
Purchasing wall-quilt panels. Wall-quilt panels are usually printed to use the entire fabric width. The panel may have a border stripe on one or both sides, or none at all. The size is most often over 30" square but not larger than 1 yard (36") long. Most wall-quilt panels have coordinating yardage that may be used to add borders to enlarge the size of the quilt (Photo 1).

Designs used in wall-quilt panels. Almost any design or motif is fair game for a wall-quilt panel. They can

Photo 1. Panels may be enlarged with coordinating fabrics.

be directional or nondirectional, and realistic or geometric (Photo 2).

Photo 2. Several wall-quilt panels are shown.

Using wall-quilt panels. Wall-quilt panels may be used as the centre of a medallion-style quilt or in combination with pillow panels to make a large bed-size quilt.

When combining a wall-quilt panel with pillow panels, the design components and sizes of both elements must be considered. The wall panel must be bordered to make it large enough to fit together with the pillow panels. Using four panels or blocks on a side creates a 48" length. The centre panel with borders had to finish at this same size. It is easy to determine that if the centre panel is 36" square finished, 12" is needed to make it fit the 48" four-block strip. That means that one 6"-wide strip or a combination of strips that equal a 6" width need to be added to each side of the centre panel.

Crib-Quilt Panels

Purchasing crib-quilt panels. Crib-quilt panels are often printed with the length across the width of the fabric so if you purchase 1 yard you get one complete panel. The size range would be 36" (or less) x 45" (or less).

Designs used in crib-quilt panels. Crib-quilt panels are designed for babies or young children. Some panels are not appropriate for older children, while others can be enlarged to be enjoyed by children sleeping in a bed other than a crib. The crib-quilt panels used for SS Rainbow (page 62) and Country Bears (page 54) are both appropriate for older children and are perfect choices for making larger quilts. Geometric designs are rarely used on crib-quilt panels, while whimsical designs, such as bears, dolls and toys, are often the motifs chosen for these panels (Photo 3).

Photo 3. Crib-quilt panels include designs children love.

Using crib-quilt panels. Crib-quilt panels are designed so that, when finished as purchased, they fit a crib. Many of the coordinating fabrics available are designed with bumper pads, curtains and other useful nursery items in mind.

If turning a crib-quilt panel into a larger bed-size quilt, the coordinating fabrics can be used with solids or tone-on-tones. By adding multiple borders, including pieced or appliquéd borders, a larger quilt could be finished in a day.

Pieced borders may be changed to fit a different centre opening by using an incremental measurement of the pieced border as an adjustment to the centre panel. Refer to SS Rainbow (page 62), which uses a 2"-square incremental border.

Lap-Quilt Panels

Purchasing lap-quilt panels. Lap-quilt panels are usually printed with the width of the panel being the width of the fabric; the length is usually 1½–2 yards.

Designs used in lap-quilt panels. The designs printed on lap-quilt panels can be either geometric or realistic. Many include multiple designs such as the fabric used for Busy

Elves (page 81) and the moose panel shown in Photo 4. Others might include a wildlife scene.

Using lap-quilt panels. Lap-quilt panels can be used in the same way as crib-quilt panels. In Busy Elves, borders were added to enlarge the size to a twin-size quilt.

Bed-Quilt Yardage

Purchasing bed-quilt yardage. Bed-quilt yardage is printed with the design repeated continuously across the width and down the length. Widths may be joined to create the desired size and additional length purchased as yardage.

Designs used in bed-quilt yardage. Many traditional quilt designs are commonly found as bed-quilt yardage, such as Double Wedding Ring, Blazing Star, Crazy Patchwork and Schoolhouse (Photo 5). The patterns shared in this book can be used for any bed-quilt yardage.

Photo 4. Multiple-design panels are commonly found as lap-quilt panels.

Photo 5. Many traditional designs are printed as bed-quilt yardage.

Using bed-quilt yardage. Bed-quilt yardage can be used in large sections as quilt centres, in border strips and cut into individual components for use as faux blocks or pieced into blocks. Starry Sky (page 67) uses sections in the borders.

Adjusting bed-quilt yardage to fit the designs. Several adjustments may be made to use any bed-quilt yardage in a medallion-style design such as those given in this chapter.

Centre the panel in the width and length of the quilt centre before cutting. If this creates an awkward break in the motif, the yardage may be split into two complete sections, and a plain vertical strip may be inserted between the sections as shown in Photo 6. Adjust the width of the strip to accommodate your panel sections. For example, if your sections are 10" wide and the pattern opening is 24", use a strip between them to make the total width of the two panel sections and strip fit the pattern opening.

Photo 6. The yardage may be split into complete sections and plain vertical strips may be inserted between the sections.

This same strategy can be used if the length does not work with your panel. Add a horizontal strip between two panel sections. Both vertical and horizontal strips may

also be added. Use a horizontal strip to fit the width of the pattern and vertical strips to join the panel sections in two rows as shown in Photo 7. Using strips in this way gives a more detailed look to the quilt centre and further disguises the "cheater-quilt look."

Photo 7. Use a horizontal strip to fit the width of the pattern and vertical strips to join the panel sections in two rows.

Do not use dividing strips wider than 6" when finished—anything wider will be too heavy-looking for the design. Instead, consider dividing the panel into three sections and inserting two strips of a smaller width as shown in Photo 8. Again, this can be used both vertically and horizontally.

Photo 8. Divide the panel into three sections and insert two strips of a smaller width.

Be sure to purchase more of the fabric than you will use as dividing strips. This option is not considered in the materials list for the samples.

Unpieced borders around the centre opening may be adjusted in width to accommodate the motif size and achieve the same total size of the centre opening when combined with the border. An unpieced border may be added around the panel to make it fit the centre opening (Photo 9).

Photo 9. An unpieced border may be added around the panel to make it fit the centre opening.

Pieced borders may be changed to fit different-size centre sections as described for crib quilts. ■

COUNTRY BEARS

A crib-quilt panel can be enlarged to fit a child- or twin-size bed for the older child.

Design | Sandra L. Hatch & Sue Harvey

Project Specifications
Skill Level: Beginner
Quilt Size: 64" x 72"
Panel Size: 34" x 42"

Materials
- 2 crib-quilt panels 34½" x 42½" (1 panel may be bordered to create the proper size)
- ¼ yard each green, red, yellow and blue mottleds
- ⅝ yard yellow print
- 1½ yards red print
- 1½ yards all-over coordinating print
- Backing 70" x 78"
- Batting 70" x 78"
- Batting and backing scraps for 3-D embellishment
- Neutral colour all-purpose thread
- Clear nylon monofilament
- Quilting thread
- Basic sewing tools and supplies and pinking shears

Project Notes
Crib-quilt panels are very popular. Usually the panel has several coordinating prints and sometimes a matching border stripe. These fabrics are designed with making bumper pads and curtains in mind. Babies are only babies for a short time, but making a bed-sized quilt from the crib-quilt panel is easy.

Choose a crib-quilt panel with a design that will grow with the child to at least school age. The example here has bears in a primary-colour theme.

Purchase some coordinating prints and solids or tone-on-tones for the borders.

The sample shown has an added bonus for the smaller child. Several 3-D shapes are stitched to the quilt top to help make the quilt a fun bed companion. Each night before snuggling in for bed, the child can make a game of finding the letters and shapes. One of the shapes was left unstitched at the top edge creating a secret pocket to hide something special.

Cutting
Trim one crib-quilt panel to 34½" x 42½" for A. *Note: On the sample, trimming the panel left an even blue-and-white border that appears to be added to the quilt centre but is actually part of the original panel.*

Cut two each 1½" x 42½" B and 1½" x 36½" C strips red print.

Cut two 2½" by fabric width strips each green, blue, red and yellow mottleds for pieced D strip.

Cut four 3½" x 3½" squares red print for E.

Country Bears

Cut and piece two 1½" x 50½" F strips and two 1½" x 44½" G strips red print.

Cut and piece two 3½" x 52½" H strips and two 3½" x 50½" I strips yellow print.

Cut and piece two 1½" x 58½" J strips and two 1½" x 52½" K strips red print.

Cut and piece two 6½" x 60½" L strips and two 6½" x 64½" M strips all-over coordinating print.

Country Bears
Placement Diagram
64" x 72"

Cut seven 2¼" by fabric width strips red print for binding.

Piecing the Top

Sew B to opposite long sides and C to the top and bottom of A; press seams toward B and C.

Join one strip each green, blue, yellow and red mottleds, in that order, with right sides together along length; press seams in one direction. Repeat for two strip sets.

Subcut strip sets into 3½" D units as shown in Figure 1; repeat for 22 D units.

Figure 1

Join six D units and remove two segments from the pieced strip as shown in Figure 2; repeat for two strips. *Note: Refer to the Placement Diagram for colour order of strips. It does not matter which colours are removed.* Sew the pieced strip to opposite long sides of the pieced centre; press seams away from D strips.

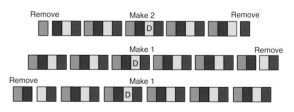

Figure 2

Join five D units and remove two segments from the pieced strip, again referring to Figure 2; repeat for two strips. Sew E to the end of each strip; press seams toward E.

Sew the pieced strips to the top and bottom of the pieced centre; press seams away from D strips.

Sew F to opposite long sides and G to the top and bottom of the pieced centre; press seams toward F and G.

Sew H to opposite long sides and I to the top and bottom of the pieced centre; press seams toward H and I.

Sew J to opposite long sides and K to the top and bottom of the pieced centre; press seams toward J and K.

Sew L to opposite long sides and M to the top and bottom of the pieced centre; press seams toward L and M.

Completing the Quilt

Prepare for quilting and quilt as desired by hand or machine referring to page 13 for instructions.

Bind edges of quilt using the previously cut red print strips referring to page 13 to finish.

Select several motifs from the remaining panel that will be easy to cut out to create 3-D shapes. *Note: On the sample, one bear head, the cat, apple, block and letters were chosen.*

Cut the shapes from the second panel, leaving a margin around each one; do not destroy the panel as other parts may be used as scraps in future projects.

Cut a batting and backing piece using the cutout shapes as patterns.

Sandwich the batting shape between the cutout shape and backing piece; pin to hold.

Sew around the edge of the design shape using clear nylon monofilament in the top of the machine and all-purpose thread in the bobbin (Photo 1).

Photo 1

Trim close to stitching using pinking shears to create ragged edges (Photo 2). Repeat for all motifs.

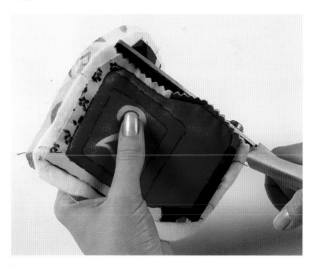

Photo 2

Lay the stitched motif on the finished quilt top over the same motif in the quilt (Photo 3); pin or baste to secure.

Photo 3

Stitch around motif using the same thread and stitch size along previous line of stitching to secure motifs to the quilt top (Photo 4). *Note: The top of the bear head was left unstitched to create a pocket (Photo 5).* ■

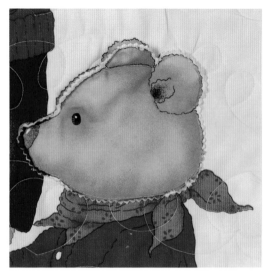

Photo 5

Tip: For different-size panels using this same design configuration, leave enough border all around or cut to a size that can be divided by two (the size of the pieced border strip units).

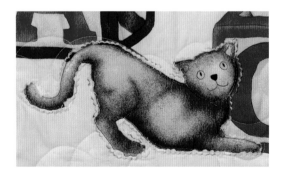

Photo 4

HEXAGON FANCY

Make the centre of a table topper in an afternoon using cheater-quilt fabric and border with triangles cut from a pillow panel.

Design | Sandra L. Hatch & Sue Harvey

Project Specifications

Skill Level: Beginner
Quilt Size: Approximately 31" x 31"
Number of Panels: 2
Pillow Panel Size: 16" x 16"
Cheater-Quilt Panel Size: 18" x 18"

Materials

⅓ yard coordinating dark print for borders
⅓ yard coordinating medium print for binding
⅝ yard cheater-quilt panel
2 (16½" x 16½") pillow panels
Backing 37" x 37"
Batting 37" x 37"
Neutral colour all-purpose thread
Quilting thread
Basic sewing tools and supplies

Project Notes

In the table topper shown, a cheater-quilt panel fabric was combined with two coordinating pillow panels. The pillow panels should be nondirectional and at least 16" x 16" square finished with a design that is usable when cut in half diagonally.

The size of the centre and the width of the fabric strips between the centre panel and the corner pillow-panel triangles can be adjusted to allow for different-size pillow panels.

If you can't find a coordinating cheater-quilt panel and pillow panels, you may use a cheater-quilt panel and a stripe or any other coordinating fabrics for the corners as shown in Photo 1.

Pillow panel and cheater yardage used in the sample project.

Photo 1. A stripe may be used instead of a pillow panel.

Instructions

Cut an 18½" x 18½" square cheater-quilt panel for centre background; fold and crease to mark centres.

Cut four 2½" x 22½" strips coordinating dark print; sew a strip to each side of the centre background, mitring corners as shown in Figure 1. Trim mitred seam to ¼" and press open as shown in Figure 2.

 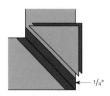

Figure 1	**Figure 2**

Select usable area of pillow panels; cut out, adding a ¼" seam allowance. *Note: The panel must be cut out as a square at least 16½" x 16½" to work in this design. Include fabric between panels on yardage to cut this size if needed. If using a stripe or coordinating fabric in place of pillow panels, cut two 16½" x 16½" squares.*

Cut each pillow panel in half on one diagonal through the centre to make four identical triangles.

Fold each triangle to mark the centre as shown in Figure 3.

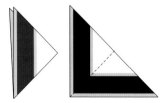

Figure 3
Fold each triangle to mark the centre.

Pin one triangle to one side of the bordered centre, matching centres; stitch. *Note: The triangle will be larger than the centre at edges.* Press seams toward triangle. Repeat for all four sides.

Lay the stitched top on a flat surface and trim triangle panel pieces ¼" beyond corners of bordered centre unit as shown in Figure 4.

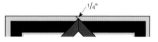

Figure 4

Prepare for quilting and quilt as desired by hand or machine referring to page 13 for instructions.

Cut four 2¼" by fabric width strips coordinating medium print for binding. Bind edges of quilt referring to page 13 to finish. ∎

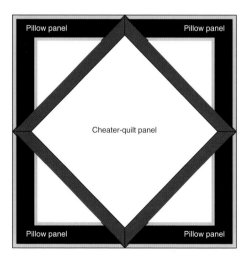

Hexagon Fancy
Placement Diagram
Approximately 31" x 31"

Hexagon Fancy

SS RAINBOW

Choose a child-motif panel with interesting details to be embellished in 3-D for a quilt any child will love.

Design | Sandra L. Hatch & Sue Harvey

Project Specifications

Skill Level: Beginner
Quilt Size: 58" x 70"
Centre Panel Size: 26" x 38" (without seams)

Materials

2 crib-quilt panels measuring at least 30" x 42"
¼ yard each 5 coordinating solids—green, gold, navy, tan and light blue (pieced strip)
½ yard coordinating check
1 yard burgundy solid (pieced strip, borders and binding)
3 yards 10"-wide coordinating border stripe
Backing 64" x 76"
Batting 64" x 76"
All-purpose thread to match fabrics
Quilting thread
Basic sewing tools and supplies

Project Notes

Fabric companies make many crib-quilt cheater panels, and usually the panels have several coordinating fabrics, including a wide border stripe. The stripe is intended to be used in curtains, bumper pads and other coordinating projects. The panels are usually the perfect size to finish for a crib-size quilt. It is also fun to create bed-size quilts using this type of panel, and many of the panels are perfect for school-age children.

The panel shown measured 36" x 46" before being trimmed for use. The outside blue dot bordering the centre design allows adjustment of the cut size of the panel.

Because the first border surrounding the centre panel is made up of 2"-square segments, the cut size of the centre panel should be divisible by 2. Cut the centre panel to include 1¼" of the blue dot all around, making the centre panel's cut size 26½" x 38½". The centre panel size can be made smaller or larger by increasing or decreasing the number of squares used in the border strips as long as the panel size can be divided evenly by 2.

Choose the same colours used in the small squares of the centre panel to create the pieced-strip border in the same colour order as on the panel. This repeats a design and colour motif from the panel. The blue dot cutaway from the centre panel is then used to border the pieced strip.

The outer border uses the wide border stripe to make a twin-size quilt for a younger child.

You can choose to add some 3-D embellishments by using gathered ragged-edge strips for the rainbow or to add manes to the animals.

SS Rainbow

What to Look For in a Panel

Look for a panel that is longer than it is wide.

Select a panel with a 3" or larger border around the centre design to allow for size changes.

Find a panel with interesting designs that can be embellished. Remember the age of the child when adding embellishments. Buttons are not appropriate for children 3 and under due to safety concerns.

Choose a panel with a matching border stripe less than 12" wide. A too-wide border overpowers the centre of the quilt.

Cut the centre panel in a number that can be evenly divided by 2.

Completing the Quilt Top

Measure and cut centre panel 26½" x 38½", saving cutaway pieces for subsequent borders. *Note: Be sure the design is centred when cutting. If necessary to make a larger or smaller centre, be sure that the size can be divided by 2. Narrow strips may be added to create the 26½" x 38½" size.*

Cut one 2½" by fabric width strip each from the five coordinating and burgundy solids.

Arrange the strips in the preferred order and stitch with right sides together along length to make a six-strip set; press seams in one direction. *Note: In the project shown, the colour order of the strips repeats the colour order of the small squares bordering the centre panel.*

Subcut the strip set into 2½" units as shown in Figure 1; repeat to make 12 units.

Figure 1

Join four units to make a side strip; press. Repeat for two side strips. Remove five segments from one end of each strip as shown in Figure 2.

Figure 2

Sew a strip to opposite sides of the centre panel; press seams away from strips.

Join three segments removed from the side strips with two units to make a top strip as shown in Figure 3; press. Repeat for the bottom strip. Sew the strips to the top and bottom referring to the Placement Diagram for positioning of strips; press seams away from strips.

Figure 3

From the strips cut away from centre panel, cut and piece two 1½" x 32½" A strips and two 1½" x 42½" B strips. Sew B to opposite long sides and A to the top and bottom of the pieced centre; press seams toward strips.

Cut and piece two 2½" x 36½" C strips and two 2½" x 44½" D strips coordinating check. Sew D to opposite long sides and C to the top and bottom of the pieced centre; press seams toward strips.

Cut and piece two 1½" x 38½" E strips and two 1½" x 48½" F strips burgundy solid. Sew F to opposite long sides and E to the top and bottom of the pieced centre; press seams toward strips.

Cut the coordinating border stripe on both sides of the fabric 10½" wide along the length of the fabric.

Lay one coordinating border stripe strip on a large flat surface. Measure a 50" length and mark with a pin; count the number of motifs that will fit in the length. Determine the centre of this number of motifs and pin. From this point, measure and mark 25¼" on each side of the pin; cut to create a 50½"-long strip with an equal amount of motif cut off each end. Repeat for two strips for G.

Repeat to cut two 38½" H strips.

Cut two 10½" x 10½" I squares from coordinating check.

Sew a G strip to opposite long sides of the pieced centre with top of border strip motif on the inside edge; press seams toward strips.

Sew an I square to each end of each H strip; sew an H-I strip to the top and bottom of the pieced centre; press seams toward strips.

Completing the Quilt

Prepare for quilting and quilt as desired by hand or machine referring to page 13 for instructions.

Cut seven 2¼" by fabric width strips burgundy solid for binding. Bind edges referring to page 13 to finish.

Embellishment Ideas

The rainbow shape on the centre background is highlighted with gathered fabric strips that, when washed, create a ragged edge. This technique was repeated on some of the animal manes.

Measure area to be covered and cut 1"-wide fabric strips in chosen colours to make a strip about twice this length. *Note: Strips may have to be joined on short ends to make required length.*

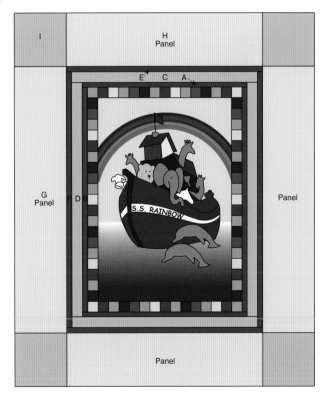

SS Rainbow
Placement Diagram
58" x 70"

Layer two strips right sides up and sew a line of gathering stitches down the centre; pull to gather strips to required length.

Centre and pin a gathered strip to the area to be covered; adjust gathers and trim excess. Stitch through the centre of the strips to secure to background.

Make clips about ⅛" apart on each side of the stitched centre of the strip as shown in Figure 4 to create a fringe. Repeat for all strips. *Note: After washing, the fringed strips will fray and create a ragged fringe (Photo 1).*

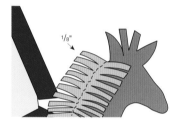

Figure 4

Wash the quilt with towels and dry to make the fringe looked ragged. *Note: Lots of lint comes off during this process; do not wash with clothing.* ■

Photo1. Close-up reveals the fringed embellishments.

STARRY SKY

Use a cheater panel as the centre of a medallion-style quilt, and continue the design using half and quarter panels in the borders.

Design | Sandra L. Hatch & Sue Harvey

Project Specifications
Skill Level: Beginner
Quilt Size: 86" x 86"
Panel Size: 14" square motifs; 32" centre

Materials
1¾ yards white print
1⅞ yards blue print
2¼ yards blue solid
4 yards cheater-quilt panel with square block motifs
Backing 92" x 92"
Batting 92" x 92"
Neutral colour all-purpose thread
Quilting thread
Basic sewing tools and supplies

Project Notes
The star design has been commonly used to make cheater-quilt panels for years. The fabric used in the sample uses the design in sashed blocks that can be separated into individual pillow-panel-type squares or used as is in an overall design (Photo 1).

The purpose of this quilt is to demonstrate how the centre panel design can be repeated in outer borders. In this case, the square-in-a-square design used as the sashing square in the panel is repeated in the corners of the wide fabric border strips.

Problems encountered can easily be overcome and are not distinct on the finished quilt. The star squares in the sample were not perfectly square. They were about ¼" off in one direction. This means that more of the border had to be included when cutting the half blocks for the borders. If you examine the quilt closely, you will see that some of the blocks have border sections showing in the seam (Photo 2).

Photo 1. Sample yardage includes sashing all around.

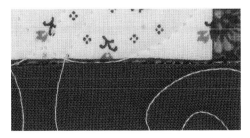
Photo 2. Look closely to see that some of the block borders show in the seam.

A second problem is that blocks would be wasted if complete half blocks plus seam allowance (Photo 3) and complete quarter blocks plus seam allowance are used for the quilt side borders and corner squares. To reduce fabric waste, use complete block halves for the sides but do not use complete block quarters for corners. The leftover half of the block can be cut back to the next design line (without added seams) to be used as corner squares (Photo 4).

Photo 3. To make half blocks with seam allowance, the other half of the block is wasted.

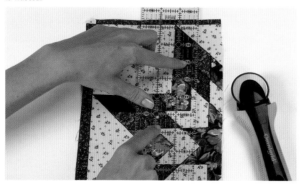

Photo 4. Corner blocks may be cut from the leftover half using the next design line plus seam allowance.

To make this quilt, begin with a 32" centre design. The blocks in the cheater quilt used here were 14" finished (more or less). Without using the included sashing around the outside of the blocks, we were able to cut the centre 32½" x 32½".

You may change the centre size to fit your panel and faux-block size. Adjust size of border and sashing strips between half blocks for other size blocks—wider for smaller blocks, narrower for larger blocks.

This type of quilt can be made in a matter of hours, and after quilting, it is hard to see that the stars aren't pieced. If the centre panel were set on point, a whole different look could be achieved as shown in Figure 1.

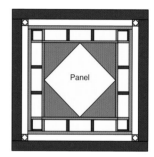

Panel

Figure 1

Instructions

Cut a 32½" x 32½" section that includes four block motifs from cheater-quilt panel fabric.

Cut two 2½" x 32½" A and two 2½" x 36½" B strips blue solid. Sew A to opposite long sides and B to the top and bottom of the panel centre; press seams toward strips.

Cut four 4½" x 36½" C strips from white print. Cut eight 4½" x 4½" D squares white print.

Starry Sky

Cut two 2½" by fabric width strips blue solid; subcut into (32) 2½" square segments for E. Mark a diagonal line from corner to corner on the wrong side of each E square.

Place an E square right sides together with D as shown in Figure 2; stitch on marked line, trim seam to ¼" and press E to the right side. Repeat on the opposite corner of D, again referring to Figure 2. Repeat on the remaining corners of D to complete a D-E unit as shown in Figure 3. Repeat for eight D-E units. Set aside four units.

Figure 2	Figure 3

Sew a C strip to opposite sides of the pieced centre; press seams toward C. Sew a D-E unit to the end of the remaining two C strips; press seams toward C. Sew a D-E-C strip to the remaining sides of the pieced centre; press seams toward D-E-C strips.

Cut and piece two 2½" x 44½" F strips and two 2½" x 48½" G strips blue solid. Sew F to opposite long sides and G to the top and bottom of the pieced centre; press seams toward strips.

Cut 16 half-panel blocks 7½" x 14½" for H.

Cut eight 1½" x 7½" I strips using blue print or leftover sashing cut from between block designs. Cut eight 2½" x 7½" J strips blue solid. *Note: Check the size needed here for your version. If you need a longer strip, cut the J pieces wider as needed. If your strip should be smaller, adjust the size of both the I and J strips to shorten.*

Join three H pieces with two I and two J strips to make a side row as shown in Figure 4; press seams toward strips. Repeat for four strips.

Figure 4

Cut four corner K squares from the leftover half panels, cutting back into the outside block design as shown in Photo 5. *Note: Don't worry about size of squares at this time.*

Photo 5. Cut corner squares as shown.

Cut eight 3" x 8" L strips blue print or leftover sashing cut from between star panel designs. Sew an L strip right sides together to one side of one K square as shown in Figure 5. *Note: The L strip will be longer than sides of K. Note direction of star point of K and be sure to sew L to the outside edges, not the inside star-point edges. Press seams toward L; trim the L strip even with K at ends as shown in Figure 6.*

Figure 5	Figure 6

Sew another L strip to the adjacent side of K; press and trim as before to complete a K-L corner unit referring to Figure 7. Repeat for four K-L units. Trim excess from the L strips to make the unit 7½" x 7½" as shown in Figure 8. *Note: Or trim to the size of the H width plus seams.*

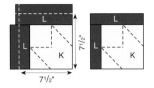

Figure 7   **Figure 8**

Sew an H-I-J strip to opposite sides of the pieced centre referring to the photo of the finished quilt for positioning of designs; press seams away from the H-I-J strips.

Sew a K-L unit to opposite ends of the remaining H-I-J strips referring to the Placement Diagram for positioning of the K-L units; press seams toward J.

Sew a pieced strip to the remaining sides of the pieced centre; press seams away from pieced strips.

Cut and piece two 2½" x 62½" M strips and two 2½" x 66½" N strips blue solid; sew M to opposite long sides and N to the top and bottom of the pieced centre. Press seams toward strips.

Cut and piece four 4½" x 66½" O strips white print. Sew an O strip to opposite sides; press seams toward O. Sew a D-E unit to each end of the remaining two O strips; press seams toward O. Sew a D-E-O strip to the remaining sides of the pieced centre; press seams toward strips.

Cut and piece two 6½" x 74½" P strips and two 6½" x 86½" Q strips blue print. Sew P strips to opposite sides and Q strips to the top and bottom of the pieced centre; press seams toward strips.

Completing the Quilt
Prepare for quilting and quilt as desired by hand or machine referring to page 13 for instructions.

Cut nine 2¼" by fabric width strips blue solid for binding. Bind edges of quilt referring to page 13 to finish. ■

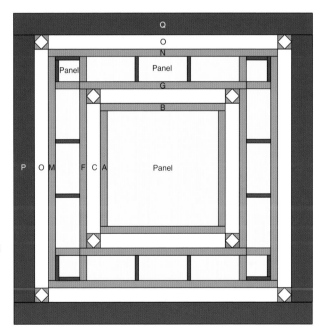

Starry Sky
Placement Diagram
86" x 86"

My Winter Garden Panel Cuddler

Stitch up a quick frayed quilt using flannel fabrics and a preprint flannel panel.

Design | Pearl Louise Krush

Project Specifications

Skill Level: Beginner
Quilt Size: 52" x 70"
Preprint Panel Finished Size: 20" x 40"

Materials

21" x 41" preprint panel
⅓ yard each 6 assorted flannel prints
½ yard rust print
2½ yards blue snowflake print flannel
4¼ yards print flannel for backing and binding
3 yards 44"-wide thin cotton batting
All-purpose thread to match fabrics
Basic sewing tools and supplies

Project Notes

Preprint panel fabrics are available in many design choices. Basic pieced, appliquéd and frayed quilts are only a few of the quilting methods open to you. Many other home decorating and clothing items can be made easily by cutting up the panel into its various components and applying the pieces to the project you are making.

Have fun making a frayed quilt using a preprint panel and its coordinating fabrics. Each seam on the quilt is sewn using ½" seams on the right side. Flannel fabric is suggested for this type of quilt because it frays better

than other cotton fabrics. The photo below shows other suggestions for using the same panel with a section applied to a purchased sweatshirt, pillow, kitchen towel and canvas bag.

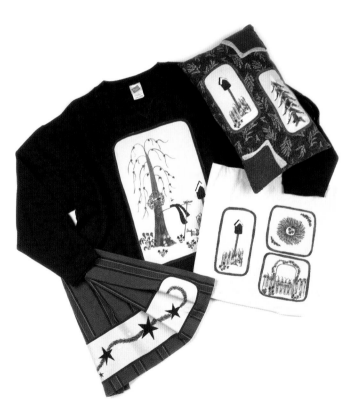

My Winter Garden
Panel Cuddler

Cutting

Cut a 22" x 42" rectangle backing print for centre panel backing; cut batting 20" x 40".

Cut two 3" x 41" B strips and two 5" x 25" C strips each rust print and backing print flannel. Cut two each 2" x 40" and 4" x 24" thin cotton batting strips.

Cut four 9" x 9" D squares from each of the six assorted flannel prints; set aside two squares of one fabric for another project.

Cut 22 thin cotton batting squares 8" x 8".

Cut six 9" by fabric width strips backing print flannel; subcut into 22 E squares 9" x 9".

Cut two 3¾" x 41" F and two 6¾" x 70½" G strips along the length of the blue snowflake print flannel. Cut and piece two strips each 3¾" x 41" F and 6¾" x 70½" G strips backing flannel print.

Cut and piece two 3¼" x 40" strips and two 6¼" x 70½" strips thin cotton batting.

Cut seven 2½" by fabric width strips from backing print flannel for binding.

Building the Quilt

Centre and place the 20" x 40" batting rectangle between the preprint panel and the 22" x 42" rectangle backing print; pin or baste to hold.

Quilt the layers as desired by hand or machine to the edge of the batting; trim the backing even with the panel top.

Note: The batting does not extend to the edges of the backing and top quilted layers.

Centre and layer the 2" x 40" batting strips between the 3" x 41" rust print and backing print B strips. Repeat this layering process with the 4" x 24" batting strips and the 5" x 25" rust print and backing C strips.

Quilt all layers as desired by hand or machine to within ½" of all fabric edges.

Sew the quilted B strips to opposite long sides of the quilted centre panel with backing pieces right sides together and using a ½" seam allowance. *Note: The seam allowance will be on the right side of the quilt and frayed when complete.*

Sew the quilted C strips to the top and bottom of the quilted centre panel in the same manner as B strips.

Layer and quilt the D and E squares and 8" x 8" batting squares in the same manner as for centre panel.

Join six quilted D-E squares to make a strip referring to the Placement Diagram for positioning of fabrics; repeat for two strips. Sew a strip to opposite long sides of the centre panel.

Join five quilted D-E squares to make a strip; repeat for two strips. Sew a strip to the top and bottom of the centre panel.

Layer the 3¼" x 40" batting strips with the F strips and the 6¼" x 70½" batting strips with the G strips, aligning one long edge of the batting strips with one long edge of the F and G strips and aligning both short edges of the G strips. *Note: The aligned edges will be the outside edges of the quilt that will later be bound.*

Quilt all layers out to the aligned edges and to within ½" of remaining edges.

Sew the F strips to the top and bottom and G strips to opposite long sides using a ½" seam allowance.

Finishing the Quilt

Join the previously cut 2½" binding strips on short ends to make one long strip for binding. Fold strip along length with wrong sides together; press.

Sew binding to quilt edge with raw edges matching, mitring corners and overlapping beginning and end; turn to the backside. Hand- or machine-stitch in place.

Clip all ½" seam allowances almost to the sewing line and clip straight lines into the corners as shown in Figure 1 to make fringe.

Figure 1

Wash the quilt in cold water; remove all excess lint from washer when cycle is complete.

Dry the quilt in a dryer. Adding a fabric softener dryer sheet will make the quilt even softer. Remove lint from dryer. Shake the quilt outside to remove excess lint

and threads. *Note: You may use a lint brush or the sticky side of a piece of wide tape to remove any remaining lint or thread.* ■

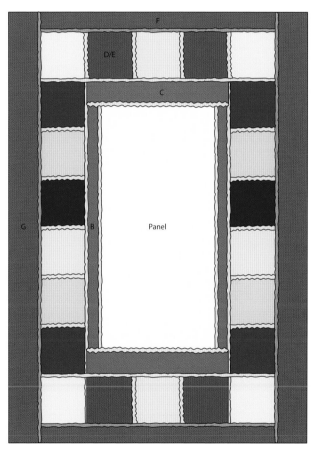

My Winter Garden Panel Cuddler
Placement Diagram
52" x 70"

STAR OF WONDER

A red zigzag frame surrounds both the stars in the blocks and the centre panel in this bed-size quilt.

Design | Sue Harvey & Sandy Boobar

Project Specifications
Skill Level: Beginner
Quilt Size: 63" x 73½"
Block Size: 10½" x 10½"
Number of Blocks: 16

Materials
1 (24" x 42") Nativity panel
⅜ yard medium green speckled
½ yard light green print
⅔ yard gold tonal
⅞ yard cream tonal
2 yards red tonal
2⅓ yards dark green print
Backing 69" x 80"
Batting 69" x 80"
All-purpose thread to match fabrics
Hand- or machine-quilting thread
Basic sewing tools and supplies

Cutting
Cut three 4" by fabric width strips light green print; subcut strips into (28) 4" A squares.

Cut six 6⅛" by fabric width strips red tonal; subcut strips into (32) 6⅛" B squares.

Cut four 2¼" by fabric width I strips red tonal.

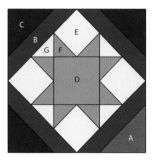

Corner
10½" x 10½" Block
Make 4

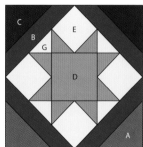

Framed Star
10½" x 10½" Block
Make 12

Cut seven 2¼" by fabric width strips red tonal for binding.

Cut four 4" by fabric width strips dark green print; subcut strips into (36) 4" C squares.

Cut four 4" by fabric width H strips dark green print.

Cut seven 5¾" by fabric width J strips dark green print.

Cut two 4" by fabric width strips gold tonal; subcut strips into (16) 4" D squares.

Cut four 2⅝" by fabric width strips gold tonal; subcut strips into (64) 2⅝" squares. Cut each square in half on one diagonal to make 128 F triangles.

Star of Wonder

Cut five 3" by fabric width strips cream tonal; subcut strips into (64) 3" E squares.

Cut two 3¾" by fabric width strips cream tonal; subcut strips into (16) 3¾" squares. Cut each square on both diagonals to make 64 G triangles.

Trim the Nativity panel ¼" from the edges of the gold scroll border to yield a 20" x 37½" rectangle.

Cut two strips each medium green speckled 1¼" x 37½" (L) and 3" x 21½" (M).

Piecing the Blocks

Mark a diagonal line from corner to corner on the wrong side of each A and C square.

Referring to Figure 1, place A right sides together on one corner of B; stitch on the marked line, trim seam allowance to ¼" and press toward A.

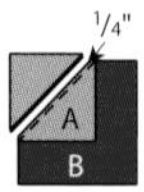

Figure 1

Repeat on the opposite corner of B as shown in Figure 2; cut B in half on one diagonal to make two A-B units, again referring to Figure 2. Repeat to make 28 A-B units.

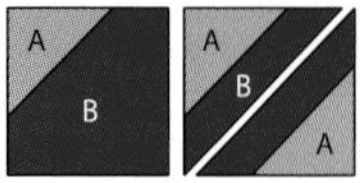

Figure 2

Repeat with B and C squares to make 36 B-C units as shown in Figure 3.

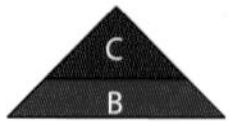

Figure 3

Sew F to two adjacent sides of each E square to complete 64 E-F units as shown in Figure 4; press seams toward F.

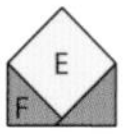

Figure 4

Sew an E-F unit to opposite sides of each D square as shown in Figure 5; press seams toward D.

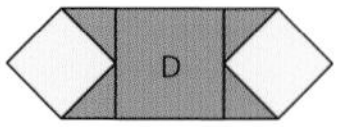

Figure 5

Sew G to the F edges of the remaining E-F units as shown in Figure 6; press seams toward G.

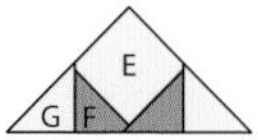

Figure 6

Sew an E-F-G unit to opposite sides of each D-E-F unit to complete the block centre units as shown in Figure 7; press seams toward the E-F-G units.

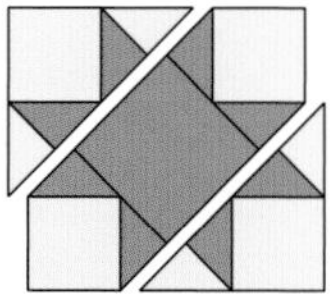

Figure 7

Sew an A-B unit to two adjacent sides and B-C units to the remaining sides of a block centre unit to complete one Framed Star block referring to the block drawing for positioning; press seams toward the A-B and B-C units. Repeat to make 12 blocks.

Sew an A-B unit to one side and B-C units to the remaining sides of a block centre unit to complete one Corner block referring to the block drawing for positioning; press seams toward the A-B and B-C units. Repeat to make four blocks.

Finishing the Quilt

Sew the L strips to opposite long sides and the M strips to the top and bottom of the trimmed panel; press seams toward strips.

Join four Framed Star blocks to make a row as shown in Figure 8; press seams open. Repeat to make two rows.

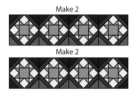

Figure 8

Sew the rows to opposite sides of the bordered panel; press seams toward the panel.

Join two Framed Star blocks and two Corner blocks to make a row, again referring to Figure 8; press seams open. Repeat to make two rows.

Sew a row to the top and bottom of the bordered panel; press seams toward the panel.

Join the H strips on short ends to make a long strip; press seams to one side. Cut the strip into two 63½" strips.

Repeat the previous step with the I strips.

Repeat again with the J strips to cut four 63½" J strips.

Sew an H strip to an I strip to a J strip; press seams away from I. Repeat to make two pieced strips.

Sew a pieced strip to opposite long sides and the remaining J strips to the top and bottom of the pieced centre to complete the top; press seams toward the pieced strips and J.

Layer, quilt and bind referring to Finishing Your Quilt on page 13. ■

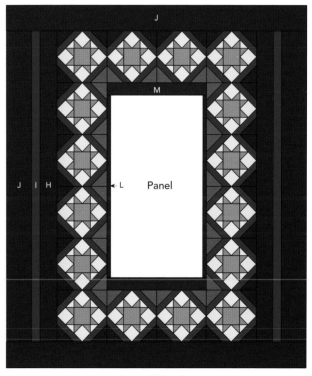

Star of Wonder
Placement Diagram 63" x 73½"

Busy Elves

BUSY ELVES

Cut up a cheater-quilt panel designed with a variety of framed motifs to create a larger bed-size quilt.

Design | Sandra L. Hatch & Sue Harvey

Project Specifications
Skill Level: Intermediate
Quilt Size: 66" x 77"

Materials
1 lap-quilt panel with a variety of large framed motifs
¼ yard each coordinating green, cream and blue prints
⅝ yard coordinating burgundy print for binding
½ yard patchwork motifs with squares
¾ yard green mottled
2¼ yards coordinating squares print
3 yards multidesign stripe panel
Backing 72" x 83"
Batting 72" x 83"
Neutral colour all-purpose thread
Quilting thread
Basic sewing tools and supplies and graph paper

Project Notes
The lap-quilt panel used as the design basis for this quilt consisted of many different-size framed designs (Photo 1). One could add borders to this pretty panel and quilt it to make it into a bed-size quilt, but it is more fun to create something unique and different from the original panel.

Photo 1. The panel is shown before being cut.

Each motif in the original panel was isolated and cut out, adding a ¼" seam allowance all around (Photo 2 on page 82). The tallest design measured 10". This determined the panel height. The width could be any size.

Photo 2. Isolate motifs to cut.

The instructions given include making panel strips that are 10" x 32" finished. The motifs were separated by strips of coordinating fabrics to create a crazy-patchwork look. It would not be practical to include specific instructions to create each of the patchwork strips because your cheater panel will include different sizes. However, we have included the instructions to piece one strip as an example of how you may create your own version.

A stripe panel includes several different-width stripes that can also be isolated and used for borders (Photo 5). The tree, elf train and toy border strips were all cut from the same stripe fabric. This type of stripe adds a variety of design motifs in different sizes and colours without purchasing many different fabrics.

The outside borders were carefully removed from the cheater panel and used in the patchwork strips (Photos 3 and 4).

Photo 3. The cheater panel border should be carefully removed.

Photo 4. Sections of the cheater panel border were used in the patchwork strip.

Photo 5. This multidesign stripe panel has lots of different designs.

The cheater panel used here has a variety of coordinated prints and a wide border stripe. These fabrics are integrated with the panels and used on the borders to result in a fun coordinated quilt for the holidays.

Creating Patchwork Panels

Measure the framed motifs on the lap-quilt panel to determine the height of the largest unit. Your panel has to be at least this size or larger in height. The sample uses a 10" finished height; all instructions will be based on this size.

Isolate each framed motif in the cheater panel; cut out adding a ¼" seam allowance.

Divide the number of cut motifs into four rows. *Note: The sample shown has several rows with two motifs combined with sections of the border stripe panel and the patchwork motifs with squares.*

Begin designing one row at a time. *Note: Instructions will be given here for one row as an example of how to begin.*

To piece one row, cut one strip coordinating squares print 2¼" x 10½" for A and one panel motif 5" x 10½" for B; sew A to B as shown in Figure 1. Press seam away from panel motif.

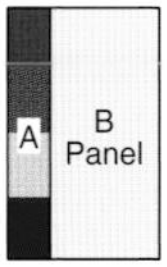

Figure 1

Cut one rectangle 3½" x 4" burgundy print for C and one rectangle 3½" x 7" for D. Sew C to D on the 3½" side; press seam in one direction. Sew to the right side edge of the A-B unit as shown in Figure 2.

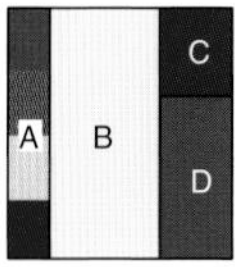

Figure 2

Cut one 9¾" x 9¼" panel motif piece for E and one 1¾" x 9¾" strip cream print for F. Sew F to the top of E as shown in Figure 3; press seam toward strip.

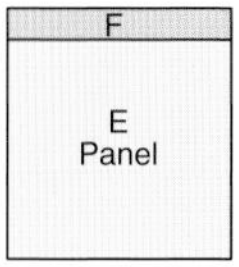

Figure 3

Cut one 3½" x 10½" strip green print for G; sew G to the E-F unit as shown in Figure 4.

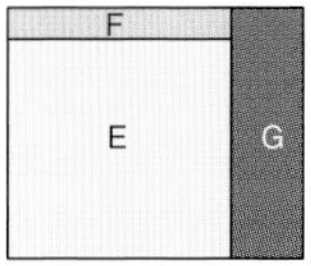

Figure 4

Cut one 7¼" x 8½" panel motif rectangle for H and one strip 2¼" x 8½" coordinating squares print for I; sew I to H as shown in Figure 5.

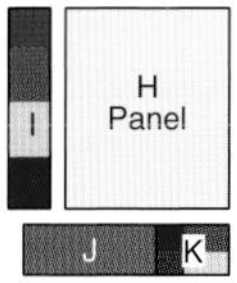

Figure 5

Cut one 2½" x 6½" rectangle burgundy print for J and one 2½" x 3" rectangle coordinating square print for K. Sew K to the 2½" end of J; press seam toward J.

Sew the J-K unit to the H-I unit, again referring to Figure 5.

Cut one 2½" x 10½" strip green print for L.

Arrange pieced units with L as shown in Figure 6 and join to complete one strip. Measure the strip to check for size; it should measure 10½" x 32½".

Figure 6

Using graph paper, create three more rows filling in sizes of framed motifs; add fill-in pieces using desired sizes to create three more panel strips, each with different layouts. *Note: The panel strips may be made larger and trimmed to size as long as framed motifs are not destroyed in the process.*

Stitch the three panel strips as desired; trim each strip to 10½" x 32½" if necessary.

Completing the Quilt

Cut five 1½" x 32½" strips green mottled for M. Join the M strips with the panel strips referring to the Placement Diagram; press seams toward M.

Cut three 1½" by fabric width strips green mottled; join the strips on the short ends to make one long strip. From this strip, cut two 45½" strips for N. Sew N to opposite long sides of the pieced centre; press seams toward N.

Cut two strips each 2½" x 38½" for P and 2½" x 45½" for O along the length of the coordinating squares print; sew O to opposite long sides and P to the top and bottom of the pieced centre. Press seams toward O and P.

Select two 4"-wide stripe sections from the multi-design stripe panel. *Note: The sample uses two different sections: the trees stripe on the sides and the toy motifs stripe on the top and bottom.* Cut two strips each

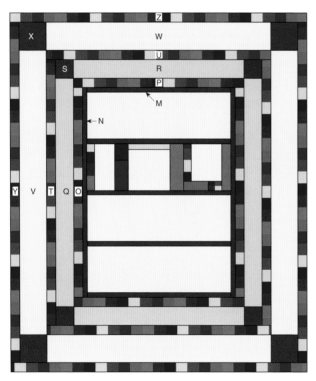

Busy Elves
Placement Diagram
66" x 77"

4½" x 38½" for R and 4½" x 49½" for Q. Cut four 4½" x 4½" squares green mottled for S.

Sew Q to opposite sides of the pieced centre; press seams toward Q. Sew S to each end of each R strip; press seams toward R. Sew an R-S strip to the top and bottom of the pieced centre; press seams toward R-S.

Cut two strips each 2½" x 50½" for U and 2½" x 57½" for T along the length of the coordinating squares print; sew T to opposite long sides and U to the top and bottom of the pieced centre. Press seams toward T and U.

Cut two strips each 6½" x 50½" for W and 6½" x 61½" for V along the length of the multidesign stripe panel. Cut four 6½" x 6½" X squares green mottled. Sew V to opposite long sides of the pieced centre; press seams toward strips. Sew X to each end of each W strip; press seams toward W. Sew a W-X strip to the top and bottom of the pieced centre; press seams toward strips.

Cut two strips each 2½" x 66½" for Z and 2½" x 73½" for Y along the length of the coordinating squares print. Sew Y to opposite long sides and Z to the top and bottom of the pieced centre; press seams toward Y and Z.

Prepare for quilting and quilt as desired by hand or machine referring to page 13 for instructions.

Cut eight strips burgundy print 2¼" by fabric width for binding. Bind edges of quilt referring to page 13 to finish. ■

COMBINATION PANELS

Our definition of a combination panel is a fabric that is made up of different same-size or random-size sections.

We separate combination panels into three different types. The first type includes random-size panel prints (Photo 1). These are made up of many different-size motifs, usually framed or separated by printed strips, lines or plain fabric.

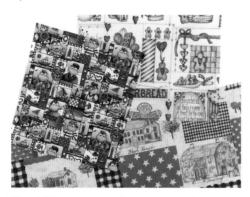

Photo 1. These fabrics are examples of random-size panel prints.

Photo 2. These fabrics are examples of preprinted, same-size motifs.

The second type includes preprinted, same-size motifs (Photo 2). The panel is printed with the same-size motifs (usually squares or rectangles) evenly spaced across the width and down the length of the yardage.

The last type includes stripe panels comprised of several various-width sections that run along the length of the fabric (Photo 3).

Photo 3. These fabrics are examples of stripe panels comprised of several various-width sections that run along the length of the fabric.

As with other types of panels, each one of the combination types has some specific information that will help you while using them in projects.

Random-Size Panel Print

A random-size panel print is a fabric printed with motifs of different sizes in an all-over design. Sometimes the motifs are distinctly separated by printed lines or open fabric space, and sometimes one motif flows into the next. Christmas Crazy (page 114) uses a random-size panel print.

Choosing random-size panel prints. Look for a print with random-size motifs that are not too small. The motifs should be large enough to be recognizable at a short distance rather than at close range. There should be space between each motif to allow them to be separated from each other (Photos 4 and 5).

Photo 4. These random-size motifs are spaced to allow cutting individual motifs and large enough to be seen from a distance.

Photo 5. These random-size motifs are too close together to cut apart and too small to use as the focus of a project.

Using a random-size panel print. Random-size prints with small motifs may be cut randomly to use in block piecing. Unless the motifs are very small, this strategy does not work well as the motif designs are usually cut into pieces too small to retain their identity (Photo 6). It is impossible to separate the motifs from the rest of the panel.

Photo 6. The motifs in this fabric will not retain identity when cut into smaller pieces.

However, many pieced-block designs include a square piece in the centre. These centres are perfect to feature fussy-cut motifs from a panel. The chosen motif may be centred in the block centre without regard to other elements of the panel that may be included (Photo 7).

Photo 7. The motif may be centred in the centre square without regard to other elements of the panel that may be included.

Another alternative is to isolate motifs in the panel for use in fusible appliqué (Photo 8).

Photo 8. Isolate motifs in the panel for use in fusible appliqué.

Fussy-cutting random-size panel motifs. It is helpful to choose a motif that is close in size to the square. This will make the motif the focus of the square (Photo 9). A motif that is much smaller than the square will not stand out and will simply become one more element of the panel shown in the square (Photo 10). A motif that is much larger than the square will look odd, as many parts of it will be cut off or included in the seam allowance (Photo 11).

Photo 9. The motif is close in size to the centre square.

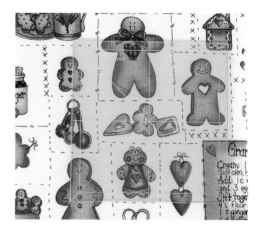

Photo 10. This motif is too small to be the focus of the square.

Photo 11. This motif is too large to fit in the square.

Both clear templates and acrylic squares can be used to help fussy-cut panel squares. Clear templates are centred over the motif, marked around, and then the square is cut out with scissors (Photo 12). Various sizes of acrylic squares are useful for fussy-cutting panel motifs. The appropriate-size square is centred over the motif and cut around using a rotary cutter (Photo 13).

Photo 12. Centre the template over the motif and mark around the template.

Photo 13. Centre the acrylic square over the motif and rotary-cut.

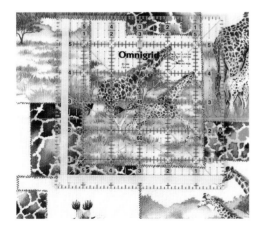

Photo 14. Centre the motif within the masked-off square.

An all-purpose acrylic square may also be used to fussy-cut the motifs. Mask off the required cut size on the square. Place the square on the motif, centring the motif within the masked-off area (Photo 14). Cut two sides of the square (Photo 15). Turn the square, realign the edges of the square with the previous cuts and cut the remaining two sides (Photo 16).

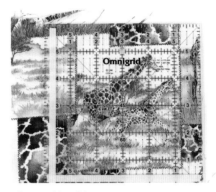

Photo 15. Cut two sides of the square.

Photo 16. Realign the square and cut the remaining sides.

Rotary-cutting the squares is much faster and more accurate than the template method, since there are no variations in line width to contend with. However, for all methods, each square must be individually cut.

Preprinted Same-Size Motifs

A preprinted same-size motif is a fabric panel made up of same-size motifs—usually squares or rectangles—evenly spaced across the width and down the length of the yardage (Photo 17). Most projects in this book use preprinted same-size squares, referred to as preprint squares. The following information specifies preprint squares but is also applicable to other shapes.

Projects that use preprinted same-size motifs include Wild Safari World (page 101), Best Friends Log Cabin (page 96) and Bear Treats (page 110).

Photo 17. Same-size motifs are printed on these fabrics.

Choosing preprinted same-size squares (or motifs). Preprinted same-size squares can be found in many sizes ranging from as small as 1" up to 14". The medium and larger sizes are easy to use for things such as blocks in a quilt, the centre of blocks, border corner squares or sashing squares.

Panels made up of preprint squares are intended to be used whole as a quick quilt. For this reason, fabric companies don't consider the space between them for use as a seam allowance.

Often the squares are not printed with enough space between them to allow cutting and using adjacent squares, or the edges are butted against each other with no area between to use as a seam allowance. The seam allowance must come from the adjacent squares—you have to waste every square around the chosen one (Photo 18). This means you will have to waste nine squares around each one that you use in order to add a ¼" seam allowance. For example, to use a 3½"-finished square, you would use the equivalent of a 6½"-finished square. This means you would need at least double the amount of fabric to yield the same number of squares.

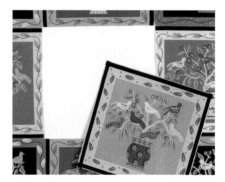

Photo 18. Many fabric sections are wasted if the preprint panels have no separation for use as seam allowance.

Using preprinted same-size squares (or motifs). Many preprint squares are not printed in a standard size that lends itself to rotary cutting. For example, a square might measure 4³⁄₁₆" instead of 4" or 4½" (Photo 19). If you want to use a fabric with this problem, adding narrow borders all around to make the square larger works. The problem is that you really need to add borders that are at least 1" all around to avoid very narrow strips. It is easier to add wider-than-needed strips and then cut the bordered square to the appropriate size (Photo 20).

Photo 19. This panel square does not measure an even size for cutting.

Photo 20. Add wider strips than needed and trim to size.

Problems encountered while using any preprinted same-size motifs or squares. Although preprint squares are sometimes difficult to work with, they are worth the effort when using them as the focal point in the centre of a block to create a mood for the finished project. Typical problems include size variations, different-size sides and no seam allowance included between squares as mentioned in "Choosing preprint same-size squares (or motifs)" (page 90).

Usually the size of the preprint squares or motifs is not accurate from one square to the next. Some of the message borders on this print are wider than others, making it hard to use the edge of the message as the

cutting line (Photo 21). In order to use the preprint as a square, this discrepancy has to be ignored.

Photo 21. Some of the message borders on this print are wider than others, making it hard to use the edge of the message as the cutting line.

You will find that working with preprint squares means finding ways to cut the squares to a common, even size that will be usable in a quilt design. You should also be aware that the end result may not be perfectly even units.

Preprint squares with plain wide fabric strips between them are very easy to adjust. Simply decide on the size that most closely equals the size of the printed square (a little larger is better) and cut out, adding a ¼" seam allowance all around (Photo 22).

Photo 22. Cut out, adding a ¼" seam allowance all around.

For squares printed without enough plain fabric between them or for those that are much smaller than needed, cut out the squares as printed leaving a ¼" seam allowance all around. Add a 2"–4"-wide strip to each side and trim the block to the desired size. Unless using very large preprint squares—12" or larger—do not add strips wider than 4" to avoid overshadowing the square.

Because the squares are not perfectly square or evenly printed on the fabric, the space between them varies. Cutting them apart does not always leave the same amount of background fabric for seam allowance all around (Photo 23). Offset the uneven look of the squares by using fabrics that match the colours in the outer edges of the finished squares (Photo 24). This blurs the seam lines between the panel squares and the adjacent squares, making the uneven edges unnoticeable. This can be done with any panel square that does not have a solid black outline around its edges (Photo 25). You can plan your seam line to fall just inside the black outline to use this method with any square (Photo 26).

Photo 24. Using coordinating fabrics in adjacent squares blurs the uneven look of the panel square.

Photo 25. This panel square has a distinctive black outline.

Photo 23. The background fabric is not even all around the square.

Photo 26. Stitch just inside the black outline to use this panel.

Problems encountered while using small preprint squares (or motifs). Because preprint squares are usually not really square and must be cut with varying widths of background fabric, placing small squares in several places in a pieced block does not yield an attractive result. The background fabric edges make the squares look crooked in an otherwise precisely pieced block (Photo 27). Of course, the alternative is to cut the square smaller than its printed edges and eliminate the background fabric. If the square is already small, there is usually very little or no border included in the square—so, cutting them smaller often cuts into the motif, making this a poor solution. Instead, leave background fabric around the preprint motif and add fabric strips to square up the motif for use in piecing (Photo 28).

Photo 28. Cutting into small squares often destroys parts of the motif as shown in the top square. Leaving background sections and adding fabric strips to square up is a better alternative, as shown in the remaining two squares.

Photo 27. The centre square looks uneven in this pieced block.

Another problem with small preprint squares is waste. To use them in a bed-size quilt, or even in a small crib quilt, you will need to use a large number of the squares. It is difficult to find a panel with small squares printed ½" or more apart. Because this type of panel is intended to be made into a quilt by simply adding a batting and backing, widely spaced squares on the fabric would look out of balance. Be aware that there will almost always be a lot of waste when fussy-cutting small squares for individual use in a design.

Stripe Panels

We define a stripe panel as one that is made up of several various-width sections that run along the length of the fabric.

Projects that use a stripe panel include Bear Treats (page 110), SS Rainbow (page 62) and Busy Elves (page 81).

Choosing stripe panels. Stripe panels are available with directional and nondirectional motif stripes. Consider the way the stripe will be used when purchasing the stripe panel. For example, directional stripes are appropriate for top and bottom borders of a wall quilt, but difficult to use on the sides of the same quilt. Look for a panel that includes both styles of stripes for the most versatility.

Using stripe panels. There are several things to consider when using stripe panels as borders on quilts. First, how should the stripe be oriented on the quilt edges? Will the quilt be used on a bed with the sides and the bottom hanging over the edge of the bed? Are there directional and nondirectional sections of the stripe? Can the stripe be divided into four equal-width sections for use on the sides, top and bottom of the quilt? How will the side borders join with the top and bottom borders? Will there be corner squares in the border?

A stripe used for the top and bottom borders should be oriented upright on a wall quilt. If the quilt is to be placed on a bed with the border hanging over the edge, a directional stripe should be placed so that it is upright when viewed on the side of the bed—the top of the stripe should be placed toward the centre of the quilt (Photo 29). If the quilt is not a bed size, a directional stripe can be cut as a cross-section for use as side borders (Photo 30).

This allows you to place all borders in an upright position on the quilt.

Photo 29. The directional stripe is upright when hanging over the edge of the bed.

Photo 30. A cross-section of border strip may be used for side borders.

If a stripe panel has both directional and nondirectional sections, the directional sections can be used for the top and bottom, the nondirectional sections for the sides. Many times the nondirectional sections are narrower than the directional section. This is easily remedied by adding a coordinating fabric strip to the nondirectional stripe strip, to increase the overall width of the border to match the size of the directional stripe strip (Photo 31).

Photo 32. Use a corner square or fabric strip as a break between side and end borders.

Photo 31. Use a corner square or fabric strip as a break between side and end borders.

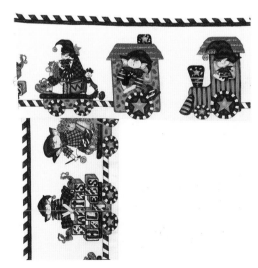

Photo 33. A busy end border looks awkward when butted against a busy side border.

The wide stripes used for the top and bottom border on Bear Treats (page 110) included a section of water on the bottom edge of the top border and on the top edge of the bottom border. This serves as a good break between these borders and the side borders. If your stripe does not have a plain-looking area to use as a break, a border corner square can be used or a plain fabric strip can be added to the top and bottom borders (Photo 32). This will prevent the awkward break when a busy side border joins to an equally busy top or bottom border (Photo 33). ∎

BEST FRIENDS LOG CABIN

Preprint squares make perfect centres for Log Cabin blocks.

Design | Sandra L. Hatch & Sue Harvey

Project Specifications
Skill Level: Beginner
Quilt Size: 73" x 87"
Block Size: 14" x 14"
Number of Blocks: 20
Panel Size: 8" x 8"

Materials
(20) 8½" x 8½" preprint squares (A)
⅞ yard red mottled
1⅛ yards geometric print (dark 1)
1¼ yards yellow print (light 1)
1¼ yards blue-and-white check (light 2)
2¼ yards dark blue print (dark 2)
Backing 79" x 93"
Batting 79" x 93"
Neutral colour all-purpose thread
Quilting thread
Basic sewing tools and supplies

Project Notes
Any size preprint square or rectangle may be used as the centre of Log Cabin blocks. It doesn't matter what size they are—they can even be different sizes.

The squares used in the sample finish at 8" x 8". They are directional—the designs should appear in an upright position on the finished quilt (Photo 1).

Photo 1. The sample yardage for this project included 8" preprint squares.

The instructions are given to finish the quilt as shown using an 8"-square centre with blocks to finish at 14"-square. You may use a larger or smaller centre-square design and keep strip sizes the same to make a different-size block, or you may adjust the size and number of strips to create a 14"-square block.

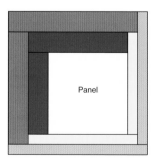

Log Cabin Variation
14" x 14" Block
Make 20

Best Friends
Log Cabin

The pieced segments used in the borders are 1" finished, making it easy to add or subtract segments to fit different-size quilts.

The method used to create the Log Cabin Variation blocks is simple and quick. Using large preprint square centres makes it possible to piece the centre of the top in no time. The pieced border takes a little time, but is worth the effort to make a pretty quilt.

Cutting

Cut 1½" by fabric width strips as follows: 27 strips yellow print (B), 17 strips blue-and-white check (C), five strips red mottled (D) and 10 strips dark blue print for E.

Cut 2½" by fabric width strips as follows: nine strips dark blue print (F) and 14 strips geometric print (G).

Cut and piece one 1½" x 57½" H strip, one 1½" x 70½" I strip, two 1½" x 65½" J strips and two 1½" x 77½" K strips blue-and-white check.

Cut and piece two each 4½" x 73½" L and 4½" x 79½" M strips dark blue print.

Cut eight 2¼" by fabric width strips red mottled for binding.

Piecing Blocks

Lay an A square right side down on an F strip with top of A at the top of the strip as shown in Figure 1; stitch. Continue adding A squares to the F strip until the strip is used up. Repeat for all A squares.

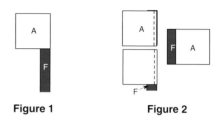

Figure 1   **Figure 2**

Trim F strips even with A as shown in Figure 2; press F to the right side, again referring to Figure 2.

Lay the A-F units on another F strip with the F strip at the bottom as shown in Figure 3; stitch. Continue adding A-F units to the strip until the strip is used up. Repeat for all A-F units.

Figure 3

Trim the A-F units and press to complete A-F units as shown in Figure 4.

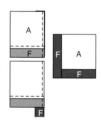

Figure 4

Continue adding strips, trimming and pressing in this method referring to Figure 5 for order of piecing to complete 20 blocks.

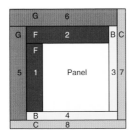

Figure 5

Completing the Quilt

Arrange the blocks in four rows of five blocks each, keeping centre A squares upright. Join blocks to make rows referring to Figure 6; press seams in opposite direction in alternating rows.

Figure 6

Join the rows to complete the pieced centre; press seams in one direction.

Sew an I strip to the left long side and H to the top of the pieced centre; press seams toward strips.

Sew a D strip between two B strips with right sides together along length; press seams toward D. Repeat for five strip sets.

Subcut B-D strip sets into 1½" segments as shown in Figure 7. You will need 134 B-D segments.

Sew a B strip between two E strips with right sides together along length; press seams toward B. Repeat for five strip sets.

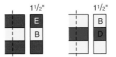

Figure 7

Subcut B-E strip sets into 1½" segments, again referring to Figure 7. You will need 134 B-E segments.

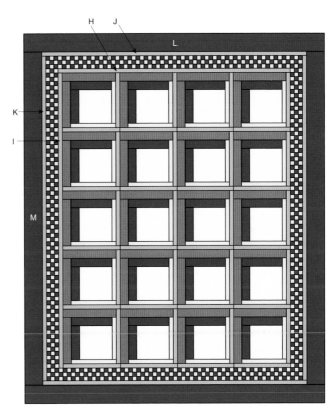

Best Friends Log Cabin
Placement Diagram
73" x 87"

Join 36 B-D and 35 B-E segments to make a strip, alternating placement of segments as shown in Figure 8; press seams in one direction. Repeat for two strips.

63

71

Figure 8

Sew a strip to opposite long sides of the pieced centre; press seams away from the pieced strip.

Join 31 B-D and 32 B-E segments to make a strip, alternating placement of segments, again refer- ring to Figure 8; press seams in one direction. Repeat for two strips.

Sew a strip to the top and bottom of the pieced centre; press seams away from the pieced strip.

Sew K strips to opposite long sides and J strips to the top and bottom of the pieced centre; press seams toward strips.

Sew M strips to opposite long sides and L strips to the top and bottom of the pieced centre; press seams toward strips.

Prepare for quilting and quilt as desired by hand or machine referring to page 13 for instructions.

Bind edges of quilt using the previously cut red mottled binding strips referring to page 13 to finish. ∎

WILD SAFARI WORLD

Use preprint squares to personalize the traditional Trip Around the World design.

Design | Sandra L. Hatch & Sue Harvey

Project Specifications

Skill Level: Beginner

Quilt Size: Size varies

Panel Size: Size varies

Materials for All Sizes

Coordinating fabrics 1–6 for piecing

Coordinating fabric 7 for piecing and binding

Coordinating fabric 8 for piecing and inner border

Large print for outer border

Preprint square fabric to yield 71 squares
   (see Project Notes)

Neutral colour all-purpose thread

Quilting thread

Basic sewing tools and supplies

Project Notes

This quilt uses same-size preprint squares (see page 90 for special considerations). The traditional Trip Around the World design is unique in that there are no individual pieced blocks—the design is created with only squares. It offers a perfect opportunity to showcase preprint squares, and at the same time, camouflage their uneven edges with the fabrics in the squares that surround them. In the sample project, each square includes an animal motif surrounded by a patterned border with only about ⅜" between the squares (Photo 1). We split the panel as evenly as possible between the squares and used parts of the square border sections to make up the difference in

the seam allowance (Photo 2). In this way, we were able to use every square in the panel.

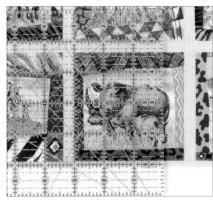

Photo 1. This panel includes about ⅜" for possible seam allowances.

Photo 2. Part of the square border sections will be included in the seam allowance.

If your preprint square does not include a border section from which to cut seam allowance, you will have to cut into adjacent squares for the seam allowance as noted in Preprinted Same-Size Motifs on page 90. For the sample project, this means that each usable 3½"-finished project square would use the equivalent of a 6½"-finished square. Instead of 1¼ yards of fabric, you would need 2½ yards.

The sample project uses a 3½"-finished preprint square to make a double/queen-size quilt. You may use this Trip Around the World design for other quilt sizes. Refer to the chart given on page 105 for yardage requirements and cutting information. The piecing instructions are the same for all sizes. The figure drawings and Placement Diagram use information for the sample project (Double/Queen).

Piecing the Centre

Join one A-B strip each fabrics 1, 2, 3 and 4 to make an A strip set as shown in Figure 1; repeat to make A strip sets as indicated in the Yardage & Cutting Chart on page 105.

A

Figure 1

Join one A-B strip each fabrics 5, 6, 7 and 8 to make a B strip set as shown in Figure 2; repeat to make B strip sets as indicated in the Yardage & Cutting Chart on page 105.

B

Figure 2

Cut the A and B strip sets into units as shown in Figure 3 referring to the Yardage & Cutting Chart for the unit size. Set aside 24 A units and 22 B units.

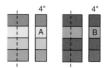

Figure 3

Separate segments from the remaining A units to make A1, A2 and A3 units and AA1, AA2 and AA3 units as shown in Figure 4. *Note: Be sure to separately stack and carefully label each unit to make piecing easier.*

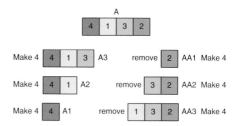

Figure 4

Separate segments from the remaining B units to make B1, B2 and B3 units, and BB1, BB2 and BB3 units as shown in Figure 5; discard two BB1 units. *Note: Be sure to separately stack and carefully label each unit to make piecing easier.*

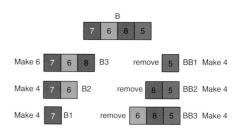

Figure 5

Wild Safari World

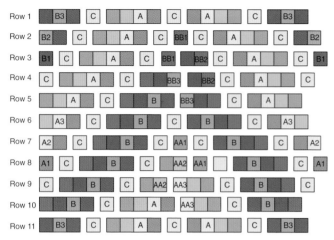

Row 1	B3	C	A	C	A	C	B3
Row 2	B2	C	A	C	BB1	C	A	C	B2
Row 3	B1	C	A	C	BB1	BB2	C	A	C	B1
Row 4	C	A	C	BB3	BB2	C	A	C
Row 5	A	C	B	BB3	C	A
Row 6	A3	C	B	C	B	C	A3
Row 7	A2	C	B	C	AA1	C	B	C	A2
Row 8	A1	C	B	C	AA2	AA1	B	C	A1
Row 9	C	B	C	AA2	AA3	C	B	C
Row 10	B	C	A	AA3	C	B
Row 11	B3	C	A	C	A	C	B3

Figure 6

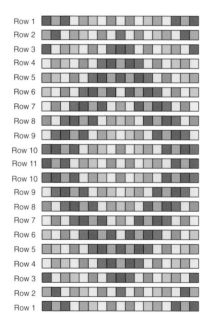

Row 1
Row 2
Row 3
Row 4
Row 5
Row 6
Row 7
Row 8
Row 9
Row 10
Row 11
Row 10
Row 9
Row 8
Row 7
Row 6
Row 5
Row 4
Row 3
Row 2
Row 1

Figure 7

Join units to make 11 different rows as shown in Figure 6; press seams in one direction. Repeat to make two each rows 1–10. You will need 21 rows total.

Join the rows to complete the pieced centre as shown in Figure 7, beginning with row 1 as the top row and adding rows 2–11 in ascending numerical order and then rows 10–1 in descending numerical order to end with row 1 as the bottom row; press seams in one direction.

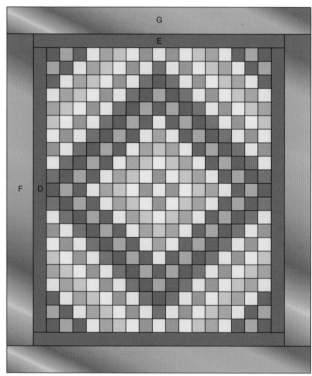

Wild Safari World
Placement Diagram
80½" x 94½"

Completing the Quilt

Sew a D strip to opposite long sides and an E strip to the top and bottom of the pieced centre; press seams toward strips.

Sew an F strip to opposite long sides and a G strip to the top and bottom of the pieced centre; press seams toward strips to complete the top. **Note:** *The king-size quilt has the G strip added to the bottom only.*

Prepare for quilting and quilt as desired by hand or machine referring to page 13 for instructions.

Bind edges of quilt using the previously cut binding strips referring to page 13 to finish. ∎

Yardage & Cutting Chart

	Crib	Twin	Double/Queen	King
Yardage Required				
Fabrics 1–6	¼ yard each	⅜ yard each	⅝ yard each	⅞ yard each
Fabric 7	½ yard	1 yard	1¼ yards	1½ yards
Fabric 8	½ yard	1 yard	1½ yards	2⅛ yards
Large Print	1⅛ yards	2 yards	2½ yards	3 yards
Preprint Squares	½ yard	¾ yard	1 yard	2 yards
Batting/Backing	42" x 48"	75" x 87"	87" x 101"	109" x 114"
Cutting Instructions				
Fabrics 1–8 for A/B	2 strips each 2" by fabric width	3 strips each 3½" by fabric width	4 strips each 4" by fabric width	5 strips each 5" by fabric width
Number of A & B strip sets	2 each	3 each	4 each	5 each
A & B unit size	2"	3½"	4"	5"
Fabric 7, 2¼" by fabric width strips for binding	4 strips	8 strips	10 strips	11 strips
Fabric 8 D strips	(2) 2" x 32"	(2) 3½" x 63½"	(2) 4" x 74"	(2) 5" x 95"
Fabric 8 E strips	(2) 2" x 29"	(2) 3½" x 57½"	(2) 4" x 67"	(2) 5" x 86"
Large print F strips	(2) 4½" x 35"	(2) 6½" x 69½"	(2) 7½" x 81"	(2) 9½ x 104"
Large print G strips cut across remaining width	(2) 4½" x 37"	(2) 6½" x 69½"	(2) 7½" x 81"	(1) 5½" x 104"*
71 C preprint squares	2" x 2"	3½" x 3½"	4" x 4"	5" x 5"

The king-size quilt uses only 1 G border strip; there is no G border on the top edge of the quilt.

All My Friends

ALL MY FRIENDS

Fussy-cut motifs from a pretty preprint fabric form the block centres in this nostalgic quilt.

Design | Rhoda Nelson

Project Specifications
Skill Level: Beginner
Quilt Size: 54¾" x 74¼"
Block Size: 7¾" x 7¾"
Number of Blocks: 35

Materials
1 yard blue print
1½ yards Overall Bill panel print (or 18 panels cut 6" x 6")
1½ yards Sunbonnet Sue panel print (or 17 panels cut 5⅞" x 5⅞")
1½ yards red-with-white polka dots
2⅓ yards yellow print
Backing 61" x 80"
Batting 61" x 80"
All-purpose thread to match fabrics
Hand- or machine-quilting thread
Basic sewing tools and supplies

Cutting
Fussy-cut 17 preprint motifs 5⅞" x 5⅞" from the Sunbonnet Sue panel print for A.

Fussy-cut 18 preprint motifs 6" x 6" from the Overall Bill panel print for B.

Cut five strips 4¾" by fabric width red-with-white polka dots; subcut strips into (34) 4¾" C squares. Cut each C square in half on one diagonal to make 68 C triangles.

Cut 14 strips 1⅝" by fabric width red-with-white polka dots; subcut six strips into (36) 6" D rectangles and eight strips into (36) 8¼" E rectangles.

Overall Bill
7¾" x 7¾" Block
Make 18

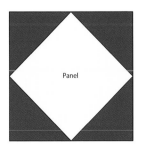

Sunbonnet Sue
7¾" x 7¾" Block
Make 17

Cut seven strips 8¼" by fabric width yellow print; subcut strips into (106) 2½" F rectangles.

Cut two strips 2½" by fabric width yellow print; subcut strips into (32) 2½" G squares.

Cut three strips 2½" by fabric width blue print; subcut strips into (48) 2½" H squares.

All My Friends
Placement Diagram
54¾" x 74¼"

Cut 14 strips 1½" by fabric width blue print; subcut strips into (384) 1½" I squares. Draw a diagonal line from corner to corner on the wrong side of each I square.

Cut seven 2¼" by fabric width strips yellow print for binding.

Completing the Blocks
Sew C to each side of A to complete one Sunbonnet Sue block as shown in Figure 1; press seams toward C. Repeat for 17 blocks.

Figure 1

Sew D to opposite sides of B; press seams toward D.

Sew E to the remaining sides of B to complete one Overall Bill block as shown in Figure 2; press seams toward E. Repeat for 18 blocks.

Figure 2

Completing the Top
Place an I square on opposite end corners of F; sew on the marked line as shown in Figure 3. Trim seam to ¼" and press I to the right side, again referring to Figure 3.

Figure 3

Repeat with I on the remaining corners of F to complete an F-I unit; repeat for 82 units. Repeat with two I squares on one end of a G square as shown in Figure 4; repeat for 28 G-I units.

Figure 4

Join three Overall Bill blocks with two Sunbonnet Sue blocks, six F-I units and two F rectangles to make a row as shown in Figure 5; press seams toward F-I units. Repeat for four rows.

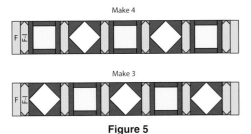

Figure 5

Join three Sunbonnet Sue blocks with two Overall Bill blocks, six F-I units and two F rectangles to make a row, again referring to Figure 5; press seams toward F-I units. Repeat for three rows.

Join two G-I units with five F-I units and six H squares to make a sashing row as shown in Figure 6; press seams toward H. Repeat for eight rows.

Figure 6

Join the block rows with the sashing rows referring to the Placement Diagram for positioning of rows; press seams toward sashing rows.

Join five F rectangles with six G-I units and two G squares to make a strip as shown in Figure 7; press seams toward F. Repeat for two strips. Sew a strip to the top and bottom of the pieced centre to complete the pieced top.

Figure 7

Finishing the Quilt

Layer, quilt and bind, referring to Finishing Your Quilt on page 13. ∎

BEAR TREATS

Combine large preprint squares with fussy-cut sashing squares and stripe panel borders to make a lap-size quilt.

Design | Sandra L. Hatch & Sue Harvey

Project Specifications

Skill Level: Beginner
Quilt Size: 55" x 70"
Panel Size: 10" x 10"

Materials

½ yard gold print
⅝ yard each light green and medium green prints
⅝ yard green/blue plaid
1 yard dark blue mottled
1 yard preprint squares with 10"-finished squares
3 yards stripe panel
Backing 61" x 76"
Batting 61" x 76"
Neutral colour all-purpose thread
Quilting thread
Basic sewing tools and supplies

Preprint squares and a coordinating stripe panel were used in the sample project.

Project Notes

Many panel fabric lines include several types of panels—random-size panel prints, stripe panels, pillow panels and preprint squares. This project uses large preprint squares and a stripe panel along with several other coordinating fabrics from the same line. The danger of using all fabrics from one line is obvious in this quilt—when complete, it resembles a preprinted panel. See Problem Solving With Pillow Panels on page 15.

For this project, it is not crucial that your stripe borders be the same width as those on the sample. Choose the stripe sections that will work for directional top and bottom borders and the nondirectional stripes for the side borders. Add a plain fabric strip to the side borders if necessary.

Cutting

Cut six 10½" x 10½" squares from preprint squares for A.

Cut three 5½" by fabric width strips light green print; subcut into (34) 3" segments for C.

Cut five 3" by fabric width strips gold print; subcut into (68) 3" square segments for D.

Cut three 5½" by fabric width strips green/blue plaid; subcut into (34) 3" segments for E.

Bear Treats

Cut and piece two strips each 2½" x 50½" for F and 2½" x 39½" for G dark blue mottled.

Cut seven 2¼" by fabric width strips dark blue mottled or binding.

Cut and piece two strips 5½" x 54½" medium green print for I. *Note: These are the strips that will be added to the* *side stripe panel borders. If your side borders are wide enough, these strips are not necessary.*

Cut two 8½" x 55½" stripe panel sections for J top and bottom borders and two 3½" x 54½" H panel stripe sections for side borders.

Fussy-cut (12) 5½" x 5½" squares from remaining stripe panel sections for B, centring a motif in each square.

Completing the Quilt

Draw a diagonal line from corner to corner on the wrong side of each D square.

Place D right sides together on one corner of C as shown in Figure 1; stitch on the marked line, trim seam allowance to ¼" and press D open, again referring to Figure 1. Repeat to make 34 C-D units.

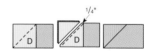

Figure 1

Repeat previous step to make 34 D-E units as shown in Figure 2.

Figure 2

Figure 3

Sew a C-D unit to a D-E unit as shown in Figure 3; press seam toward D-E. Repeat to make 34 C-D-E units.

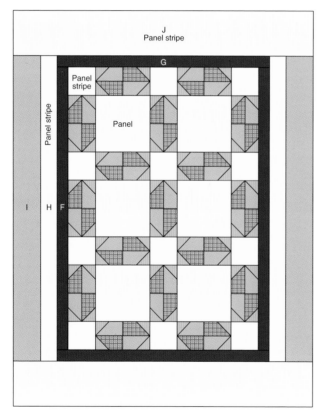

Bear Treats
Placement Diagram
55" x 70"

Join two C-D-E units to make a sashing unit as shown in Figure 4; repeat for 17 sashing units.

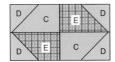

Figure 4

Join two sashing units with three B squares to make a sashing row as shown in Figure 5; press seams toward B. Repeat for four sashing rows.

Figure 5

Join two A squares with three sashing units to make a panel row as shown in Figure 6; press seams toward A. Repeat for three panel rows.

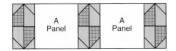

Figure 6

Join the sashing rows with the panel rows to complete the pieced centre referring to the Placement Diagram for positioning of rows.

Sew an F strip to opposite long sides and a G strip to the top and bottom of the pieced centre; press seams toward strips.

Sew I to H; press seam toward I. Repeat for two H-I strips. Sew a strip to opposite long sides of the pieced centre; press seams toward strips.

Sew a J strip to the top and bottom of the pieced centre to complete the top.

Prepare for quilting and quilt as desired by hand or machine referring to page 13 for instructions.

Bind edges of quilt using the previously cut dark blue mottled binding strips referring to page 13 to finish. ■

CHRISTMAS CRAZY

Choose any size preprint motifs as the centres of the crazy patchwork blocks. Change the colours to make a quilt with any theme.

Design | Sandra L. Hatch & Sue Harvey

Project Specifications
Skill Level: Beginner
Quilt Size: 42" x 42"
Block Size: 12" x 12"
Number of Blocks: 9

Materials
9 theme motifs for block centres
Scraps red, green and white or cream
½ yard red print for borders
½ yard green print for binding
1⅛ yards white or cream flannel for foundation
Backing 48" x 48"
Batting 48" x 48"
Neutral colour all-purpose thread
Gold metallic thread
Basic sewing tools and supplies

Project Notes
Lots of theme-print motifs can be used as featured centres of the crazy Log Cabin-type blocks (Photo 1).

Select scraps in lights, green and red for this holiday theme or simply lights and darks for other themes.

Prepare your scraps in striplike sizes, press for easy use, and you are ready to begin.

Photo 1. These motifs may be used as centres of this type of crazy-patch Log Cabin.

Today's sewing machines have lots of built-in fancy stitches. The machine we used has hundreds, and we tried over half of them on the sample quilt. You can even add seasonal messages to some blocks. What fun!

Instructions
Cut nine squares white or cream flannel 12½" x 12½" for foundations.

Centre a theme motif shape on one flannel square.

Christmas Crazy

Pin a white or cream scrap strip right sides together with the centred motif; stitch. Press the scrap strip to the right side as shown in Figure 1.

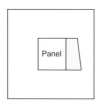

Figure 1

Add a second white or cream scrap to the top of the stitched centre and press to the right side as shown in Figure 2.

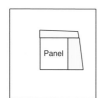

Figure 2

Continue adding scrap strips, adding red to the next side and green to the bottom of the centre. Continue adding scraps in the same colour order until the entire foundation is covered as shown in Figure 3. Trim excess even with foundation square as shown in Figure 4. Repeat for nine blocks.

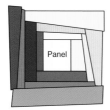

Figure 3

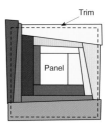

Figure 4

Using gold metallic thread in the top of the machine and all-purpose thread in the bobbin, stitch over some seams in each block using fancy machine stitches.

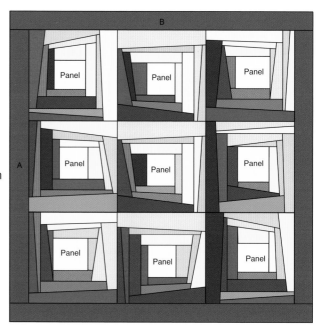

Christmas Crazy
Placement Diagram
42" x 42"

Arrange the stitched blocks in three rows of three blocks each; rearrange until satisfied with positioning. Stitch blocks together in rows; press seams in one direction. Join block rows to complete the pieced centre.

Cut two 3½" x 36½" A strips and two 3½" x 42½" B strips red print. Sew A to opposite sides and B to the top and bottom of the pieced centre; press seams toward strips.

Sandwich batting between the completed top and prepared backing piece; pin or baste layers together to hold flat.

Using gold metallic thread in the top of the machine and all-purpose thread in the bobbin, stitch over seams not previously stitched with metallic thread and in the ditch of seams between blocks and rows using fancy machine stitches (Photos 2 and 3). Stitch ¼" from seams in the border strips.

Photo 3. Use a variety of fancy stitches.

When stitching is complete, trim edges even.

Cut five strips green print 2¼" by fabric width for binding. Bind edges referring to page 13 to finish. ■

Photo 2. Fancy machine stitches can include messages.

Bugs & Butterflies

BUGS & BUTTERFLIES

Feature a large novelty print, or two or three smaller ones, in the plain sections of this quilt.

Design | Lucy A. Fazely & Michael L. Burns

Project Specifications
Skill Level: Intermediate
Quilt Size: 86" x 108"
Block Size: 22" x 22"
Number of Blocks: 12

Materials
⅛ yard purple
½ yard blue
1 yard red
1½ yards butterfly pillow panel
   (total of six 18" x 22" panels)
1⅔ yards each orange, yellow and green
2⅔ yards white solid
3 yards black print
Backing 92" x 114"
Batting 92" x 114"
All-purpose thread to match fabrics
White quilting thread
Invisible thread
2 yards 12"-wide fusible web
2 yards 22"-wide fabric stabilizer
Basic sewing tools and supplies

Instructions
Cut fabric strips 2½" by width of fabric as follows: two each black print and purple; six blue; 11 red; and 22 each orange, yellow and green.

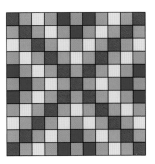

Triple Irish Chain
22" x 22" Block
Make 6

Chain Connector
22" x 22" Block
Make 6

From black print, cut two 4½" by fabric width strips and four 6½" by fabric width strips; subcut the 6½" strips into (14) 6½" x 10½" rectangles.

From white solid, cut two 22½" by fabric width strips; subcut strips into six 10½" x 22½" rectangles.

From white solid cut one fabric-width strip each 10½", 14½" and 18½".

Join 2½"-wide strips with right sides together along length to create one strip set of each combination referring to Figure 1. *Note: For best results, press seams in these and future stitched strip sets toward white, black, yellow, red and blue strips. When joining pieced segments, press seams using the fabric at ends for reference and press seams toward the same colours listed above.*

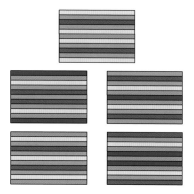

Figure 1

Subcut each strip set into twelve 2½" x 22½" segments as shown in Figure 2.

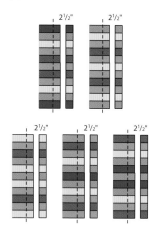

Figure 2

Join one segment each combination as shown in Figure 3 to make a section; repeat for 12 sections.

Figure 3

Cut one of each of the following 2½" by fabric width strips into two equal lengths about 22" long: red, orange, yellow, green, blue and purple. Discard one red half strip.

Piece remaining half strips into a section as shown in Figure 4.

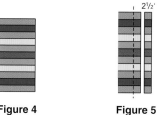

Figure 4   **Figure 5**

From this section, cut six 2½" x 22½" segments as shown in Figure 5.

Using sections and segments, piece six Triple Irish Chain blocks referring to Figure 6.

Figure 6

Using 2½" by fabric width coloured strips and white 10½", 14½" and 18½" fabric width strips, piece sections as shown in Figure 7; cut twelve 2½" segments from each section, again referring to Figure 7.

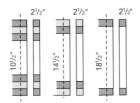

Figure 7

Join segments with the 10½" x 22½" rectangles to make six Chain Connector blocks referring to Figure 8.

Figure 8

Cut fusible web into 2"-wide strips. Roughly space the strips around the wrong-side edges of each butterfly shape. *Note: The fusible web should cover all outside edges at least ½". You may trim it so there is not more than ½" inside the butterfly edges, if desired. This method reduces the stiff areas inside the butterfly shapes, which are held in place by the machine quilting when finishing. It does not matter if the fusible web extends beyond edges, as it will be trimmed away.* Lightly fuse the strips in place, referring to the manufacturer's instructions.

Cut out each butterfly shape along the edges of the motif; remove paper backing from fusible web strips.

Centre a butterfly motif on each Chain Connector block referring to Figure 9; fuse in place.

Figure 9

Bugs & Butterflies
Placement Diagram
86" x 108"

Cut fabric stabilizer pieces to fit behind edges of butterfly shapes; pin in place.

Using invisible thread in the top of the machine, all-purpose thread in the bobbin and a narrow zigzag stitch, sew all around butterfly motifs to hold in place. When stitching is complete, remove fabric stabilizer.

Completing the Top

Join two Triple Irish Chain blocks and one Chain Connector block to make a row as shown in Figure 10; repeat for two rows.

Join two Chain Connector blocks with one Triple Irish Chain block to make a row, again referring to Figure 10; repeat for two rows.

Make 2

Make 2

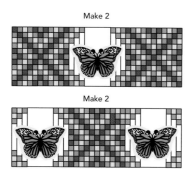

Figure 10

Join rows referring to the Placement Diagram for positioning to complete the block section.

Join remaining 2½" strips and the 4½" black print strips with right sides together along length to make strip sets as shown in Figure 11; repeat for two strip sets of each

colour group. Subcut each strip set into 2½" segments, again referring to Figure 11.

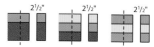

Figure 11

Join one segment from each strip set to complete an A unit as shown in Figure 12; repeat for 32 A units.

A unit

Figure 12

Join two A units and one 6½" x 10½" black print rectangle to make a B border section as shown in Figure 13; repeat for 14 B border sections.

Figure 13

Join four B border sections to make a side border strip as shown in Figure 14; repeat for two side borders.

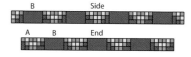

Figure 14

Join two A units and three B border sections to make an end border strip, again referring to Figure 14; repeat for two end borders.

Sew a side border to opposite sides of the block section and an end border to the top and bottom; press seams toward borders.

Cut and piece two 4½" x 86½" C strips and two 4½" x 100½" D strips black print. Sew the D strips to opposite long sides and C strips to the top and bottom of the pieced centre; press seams toward strips.

Finishing the Quilt
Prepare for quilting and quilt as desired by hand or machine.

Cut 10 strips 2¼"by fabric width black print; join strips on short ends to make one long strip. Fold strip along length with wrong sides together; press.

Sew binding strip to quilt edge with raw edges matching, mitring corners and overlapping beginning and end; turn to the back. Hand- or machine-stitch in place. ■

INDEX

Pillow Panels

INDEX

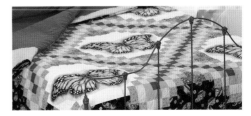

Metric Conversion Charts

Metric Conversions

yards	x	.9144	=	metres (m)
yards	x	91.44	=	centimetres (cm)
inches	x	2.54	=	centimetres (cm)
inches	x	25.40	=	millimetres (mm)
inches	x	.0254	=	metres (m)

centimetres	x	.3937	=	inches
metres	x	1.0936	=	yards

Standard Equivalents

⅛ inch	=	3.20 mm	=	0.32 cm
¼ inch	=	6.35 mm	=	0.635 cm
⅜ inch	=	9.50 mm	=	0.95 cm
½ inch	=	12.70 mm	=	1.27 cm
⅝ inch	=	15.90 mm	=	1.59 cm
¾ inch	=	19.10 mm	=	1.91 cm
⅞ inch	=	22.20 mm	=	2.22 cm
1 inch	=	25.40 mm	=	2.54 cm
⅛ yard	=	11.43 cm	=	0.11 m
¼ yard	=	22.86 cm	=	0.23 m
⅜ yard	=	34.29 cm	=	0.34 m
½ yard	=	45.72 cm	=	0.46 m
⅝ yard	=	57.15 cm	=	0.57 m
¾ yard	=	68.58 cm	=	0.69 m
⅞ yard	=	80.00 cm	=	0.80 m
1 yard	=	91.44 cm	=	0.91 m

1⅛ yard	=	102.87 cm	=	1.03 m
1¼ yard	=	114.30 cm	=	1.14 m
1⅜ yard	=	125.73 cm	=	1.26 m
1½ yard	=	137.16 cm	=	1.37 m
1⅝ yard	=	148.59 cm	=	1.49 m
1¾ yard	=	160.02 cm	=	1.60 m
1⅞ yard	=	171.44 cm	=	1.71 m
2 yards	=	182.88 cm	=	1.83 m
2⅛ yards	=	194.31 cm	=	1.94 m
2¼ yards	=	205.74 cm	=	2.06 m
2⅜ yards	=	217.17 cm	=	2.17 m
2½ yards	=	228.60 cm	=	2.29 m
2⅝ yards	=	240.03 cm	=	2.40 m
2¾ yards	=	251.46 cm	=	2.51 m
2⅞ yards	=	262.88 cm	=	2.63 m
3 yards	=	274.32 cm	=	2.74 m
3⅛ yards	=	285.75 cm	=	2.86 m
3¼ yards	=	297.18 cm	=	2.97 m
3⅜ yards	=	308.61 cm	=	3.09 m
3½ yards	=	320.04 cm	=	3.20 m
3⅝ yards	=	331.47 cm	=	3.31 m
3¾ yards	=	342.90 cm	=	3.43 m
3⅞ yards	=	354.32 cm	=	3.54 m
4 yards	=	365.76 cm	=	3.66 m
4⅛ yards	=	377.19 cm	=	3.77 m
4¼ yards	=	388.62 cm	=	3.89 m
4⅜ yards	=	400.05 cm	=	4.00 m
4½ yards	=	411.48 cm	=	4.11 m
4⅝ yards	=	422.91 cm	=	4.23 m
4¾ yards	=	434.34 cm	=	4.34 m
4⅞ yards	=	445.76 cm	=	4.46 m
5 yards	=	457.20 cm	=	4.57 m